This Book Is for You If...

☐ You have been looking for spirituality in Judaism, but you haven't been able to feel comfortable with the synagogue prayer services.

☐ You're practicing Judaism, and you want to develop an even deeper and more personal connection to God.

☐ You've felt a lack of concern for the body in your spiritual tradition.

☐ You've used meditation in your spiritual development, but you'd like a more Jewish approach to it.

☐ You're not Jewish, but you're curious about what practical spiritual resources there might be in Jewish mysticism.

If any of these statements describe you, try our approach. You'll find in this book an unusual combination of material. In each chapter, teachings about the meanings of traditional Jewish prayers provide a framework for thinking about body, mind, and soul. Second, movements choreographed to the prayers will help your body "understand" prayer. And using meditative visualizations can enhance your spiritual intent, enabling you to open the doors of deeper understanding and a more spiritual life. In the process, the ritual of prayer will become more real and significant, and so will your relationship to God.

How to Use This Book

You may find it difficult to absorb such diverse material all at once. Fortunately, you don't need to. *Minding the Temple of the Soul* can be read in bits and pieces over weeks and months. You can dip for insights into the more intellectual portions, or you can wade slowly into the depths by practicing some of the morning prayers in this new form. If you find portions difficult to understand, be patient, continue working with what you have learned, and allow your understanding to deepen and your interest to bloom.

We recommend reading the book once without trying to absorb everything. Then begin to work through it slowly.

□ Starting with the first two chapters which are relatively short, begin to practice a morning discipline of a physical and spiritual warm-up, followed by prayer with the body movements.

□ Try to make time for a meditation a couple of times a week.

□ After the first two chapters, add material from the later chapters at your own speed. You can skip around in the book to choose a meditation, study some of the explanations, or add a prayer. Chapters 3, 4, and 5 discuss the body, the mind and the soul. Chapter 6 summarizes the themes of the book and suggests how to integrate the spiritual work into all parts of your life.

In short, this is a workbook for a spiritual workout. Use it that way. You can photocopy the Prayer Wheel and the pages with the blessings and movements, and put them up on the wall near where you exercise and pray. Make copies of your favorite meditations and put them in your car for that time when you need to re-center yourself. You can also order from the publisher an audiotape with the blessings, movements, and meditations.

The more you do this work, the deeper will be your understanding of the Jewish approach to creating a balance of body, mind, and soul.

Minding
the
Temple
of the
Soul

Balancing Body, Mind, and Spirit
through Traditional Jewish Prayer,
Movement, and Meditation

TAMAR FRANKIEL & JUDY GREENFELD

FOR PEOPLE OF ALL FAITHS, ALL BACKGROUNDS

JEWISH LIGHTS PUBLISHING ■ WOODSTOCK, VERMONT

Minding the Temple of the Soul: Balancing Body, Mind and Spirit through Traditional Jewish Prayer, Movement and Meditation

Library of Congress-in-Publication Data
Frankiel, Tamar, 1946-
    Minding the temple of the soul : balancing body, mind & spirit through tradi-
        tional Jewish prayer, movement & meditation / Tamar Frankiel and Judy
        Greenfeld.
          p.   cm.
    Includes bibliographical references.
    ISBN 1-879045-64-8 (pbk.)
    1. Prayer—Judaism. 2. Meditation—Judaism. 3. Spiritual life—Judaism. 4.
Gesture in worship. 5. Gesture—Religious aspects—Judaism. 6. Judaism—
Liturgy. I. Greenfeld, Judy, 1959-. II. Title
    BM669.F65 1996   96-32990
    296.7'2—dc20   CIP

10 9 8 7 6 5 4 3 2

ISBN 1-879045-64-8 (Quality Paperback Original)

Manufactured in the United States of America
Book and cover designed by Chelsea Dippel

Published by Jewish Lights Publishing
A Division of LongHill Partners, Inc.
P.O. Box 237 / Sunset Farm Offices, Rte. 4
Woodstock, Vermont 05091
Tel: (802) 457-4000 Fax: (802) 457-4004

IN MEMORY OF MY FATHER, Gilbert Savransky, with gratitude that I am able to continue the part of you that I remember as being the most beautiful and passionate—you and your Judaism. And to my mother, Belle Savransky: Your love and belief in me have been my greatest support along this pathway.

As you both vowed, "Someday you'll thank me for this."

—from Judy

TO MY FATHER AND MOTHER, John and Ruth Sizer, whose lives of integrity and commitment shine for me always. And to my brother, Mike Sizer, whose music echoes in my ears whenever I listen for it.

—from Tamar

We dealt much in soulfulness; we forgot the holiness of the body. We neglected physical health and strength; we forgot that we have holy flesh, no less than holy spirit.... Our *teshuvah* [return] will succeed only if it will be—with all its splendid spirituality—also a physical return, which produces healthy blood, healthy flesh, mighty, solid bodies, a fiery spirit radiating over powerful muscles. With the strength of holy flesh, the weakened soul will shine, reminiscent of the physical resurrection.

—*from Rav Avraham Yitzchak Kook,* Orot *(1920)*[1]

Elu Devarim

Modeh Ani

Elohai Neshamah

Mah Tovu

The Path · Awakening

Soul · Energy

Mind · Body

Bircat HaTorah

Asher Yatzar

Prayer Wheel

Beginning the Morning with Blessings

Contents

1 ⊛ Awakening   25

2 ⊛ Entering Sacred Space   37

3 ⊛ The Gift of the Body   49

4 ⊛ Clearing the Mind   77

5 ⊛ Connecting with the Soul   95

6 ⊛ Our Walk on Earth   125

Preface

THIS BOOK DEVELOPED from exercising together—exercising our minds by learning Torah, and exercising our bodies. Tamar brought her skill in Torah studies, Judy brought her expertise in working with the body. These inner and outer workouts led us, over the years, to share our understandings of the body and the spirit. As our thoughts and our bodily awareness deepened, we decided to put into writing some of what we had learned.

Judaism's intense intellectual tradition is famous. But not many people recognize how strenuously the sages of the past worked on themselves as whole individuals, examining their emotions, spending hours in contemplation, attending to their physical health. What we found in their writings has been so helpful and so enlightening to us that we want to share it.

Jewish mystical thought has been especially important to us, because it conceives of the human being and the human body as a microcosm of the universe or, in contemporary terms, as a hologram. This tradition came to us mediated through Hasidic teachings, particularly those of the Breslov and Lubavitch schools of Hasidism, which were the lenses that helped focus our study. Our intellectual debts are too numerous to detail at length, but we want to give special thanks to Avraham Greenbaum, whose transmission of the teachings of Rabbi Nachman of Breslov continues to inspire both of us.

We are especially grateful to the other students who joined us for our Torah discussions over the years, helping to open our minds and enrich our thoughts, and to the many people in our respective communities who continually added to our understanding and encouraged our work. Among our many teachers and supporters, we can mention only a few:

Thanks from Tamar to Rabbi Chaim Dalfin for opening the world of Hasidut to me through your superb teaching of *Tanya*, one of the great classics of Hasidic philosophy, and to you and Basya for your continual encouragement of my teaching and learning. To Rabbi Avraham Czapnik for your unwavering personal support and your inspiring *divrei Torah*, which have been sparks of great light. I appreciate also the encouragement that came at just the right time from Micha Taubman, from Michael Kaufmann, and from Rabbi Nathan Lopez-Cardozo.

Thanks from Judy to Rabbi Alvin Mars and Ken Hailpern of Brandeis-Bardin Institute, to Cantor Linda Kates, and to Stephen S. Wise Temple, all of whom helped me explore new depths of understanding by offering me opportunities to teach. A special thanks also to Randl Ask.

Thanks from both of us to Connie Kaplan, who helped open new worlds for us and reminds us always of who we truly are.

To all our teachers who brought us to this point: Whatever wisdom is in this book comes from you.

Thanks to Rabbi Aaron Parry for reading portions of the manuscript, and to our editors at Jewish Lights for their careful work and encouragement.

A special thanks to Sammy Silberstein for his excellent photography.

Thanks to Meir Finkelstein, who contributed so much to the audio tape for this book, by composing for the *Mah Tovu* and *Elohai Neshamah* prayers and by accompanying us on tape throughout; to Jim DeCicco, audio engineer, for his special talents; and to Rush Recording Studios.

We want to offer a special thanks to our families, especially our loving and supportive husbands, Mike Greenfeld and Hershel Frankiel—you have gone beyond the call of duty. And thanks to our children—Sami and David Greenfeld; and Shmuel, Yaakov, Chava, Rina, and Devora Frankiel—you are our greatest teachers of true spiritual innocence and love. Always know that you are more important than our work, and that we learn more from you than from any book.

Most of all, we are grateful to the *Ribbonoh Shel Olam,* the Eternal One, Who brought us and all the parts of this work together, and showed us again and again the Divine Guidance that is the true reality of this world.

Introduction

The Soul in the Body

☐ Story of a Soul

"Soul," said God, "I have a mission for you."

A mission? The Soul thought only angels had missions. "Yes, I'm ready," the Soul said aloud.

"You will go to earth for a certain period of time," God proclaimed.

"Earth? From what the angels say, it's dark and heavy there."

"Yes, compared to where you are. One of your jobs will be to bring light there."

"How do I do that?"

"You will receive instruction," said God. "There will be time set aside for that."

"What is time?" the Soul asked.

God sighed. "It's very hard to explain, but when you're in it, you'll know it."

"Whatever you say," replied the Soul.

"You will also receive what you need to help you complete your mission," *God continued. "It will also be hard to understand at first, but you'll have plenty of time to get used to it."*

"You're talking about time again."

"All right. The point is, I am giving you something unique for your mission on earth. It is called a body."

"Thank you. But what is a body? No, I guess there's no point asking. I'll find out."

"That's right. Remember, the main thing is not to fear."

In a flash, the Soul found itself in a strange situation. It seemed to be in a kind of cave, smooth and soft all around. The energy was dense, but the Soul moved through it easily. At the same time, there was an embracing warmth, almost like being in the presence of the Creator.

Then an angel appeared, a presence of gentle light. The angel lit a candle and opened an immense book. The angel explained that the Soul was now inhabiting a body, and would soon enter into the human world as a tiny member of the human species. The Soul listened and began to understand the wondrous purposes of existence, and the special role it would have in its earthly life. The angel also gave instructions, explaining how the Soul could stay connected with the spiritual world it had temporarily left behind. The knowledge was delicious—the Soul could even taste it. The Soul felt radiant with joy.

The angel gazed sweetly at the Soul, kissed it on its upper lip, just below the nose and, before the Soul could speak, disappeared. Warm darkness surrounded the Soul, and it slipped into a deep, restful sleep.

When it awoke, the Soul realized that its body was going through a great change. There was pressure and movement. The Soul wondered what was happening, and tried to remember what the angel had said. There was something about beginning a mission—but what were the instructions the angel had given? The Soul suddenly realized its clarity of understanding was gone.

Panic rose, and the Soul wanted to escape.

"Remember, the main thing is not to fear," an inner voice said.

The Soul quieted itself. But the urge to get out was strong. As the thoughts of escape grew louder, the Soul suddenly found itself being pushed with a mighty force into what seemed to be a tunnel. In a moment it was sliding down a canal toward a glimmer of light that reminded the Soul ever so slightly of home.

What a lift that small bit of light gave the Soul! Then a breeze swept through, a delicious breath of life, followed by a vibration, a sound that came from its own body. A moment later, the body was completely embraced, held, and rocked with a gentle motion. The Soul could focus now, and saw faces and eyes, almost as sweet as the angel's. Voices, one low and one high, spoke nearby, and the happy words were like music. Those loving voices also reminded the Soul of the warmth and love of the Soul World. The Soul felt a great delight.

The surrounding energy began to settle into a calmer, more regular movement. Warmth now flowed into the body, a sweet-tasting liquid. Lips and fingers moved on soft, warm skin. The fragrances of body, milk, and fabric were a kaleidoscope, changing each moment.

The Soul was thrilled at this new beginning for its life. It poured its light into all these sensations, longing to express its surprise and happiness. Its eyes opened and sent a loving look to the eyes that gazed back with a smile.

The Soul knew that a great miracle had occurred, and sent a thankful song back to... whoever had brought it to this experience.

The Soul realized that the past, and all the places it had been, had become very hazy now. The Soul hoped it would find a way to remember.

Let's begin our journey of remembering.

Reuniting Body and Soul

The body is a beautiful gift, a vehicle through which we can bring light into the world. Unfortunately, we often treat it as an object—sometimes an object of contempt, sometimes an object of worship. We may try to pretend it doesn't exist, or even try to starve it out of existence. Or we may treat it primarily as a machine, "tuning" it with the wrenches and screwdrivers of exercise to get the body "in shape," and "fueling" it with three meals a day. If anything goes wrong, we throw in a few additives (medicines) or replace the worn-out parts (surgery).[2]

When we do become aware that we are more than machines, when we begin to have an awareness of a higher level such as soul or spirit, we may see the body as a stumbling block. We may think that it stands in the way of experiencing the higher levels of consciousness. Often we are tempted to minimize the body for the sake of spirituality, as is done in ascetic traditions by fasts and deprivations. Alternatively, we are sometimes persuaded by the delusion that if we just use "mind over matter," we can meditate ourselves into a higher state, so that we will transcend the body and not have to address its forces.

But the body cannot be beaten or starved, ignored or transcended without damaging the soul as well. Our attempts to do this are a kind of indirect suicide, for the body is a gift and an ally, not an object. Our job is to transform the denseness of the body, to enlighten it so that it

---

The Baal Shem Tov, the eighteenth-century founder of Hasidism, taught about a certain verse of Torah law: "When you see the *chamor* [donkey] of your enemy lying under its burden, you might want to refrain from helping him, but you must surely help him." (Exodus 23:5)

The Baal Shem explained that this verse is not just about donkeys and helping your enemy. It has a mystical meaning. The word *chamor* can be read *chomer* (in the Torah scroll, the vowels do not appear) which means material reality, specifically your body. The verse then means, you may want to see your body as your enemy, for it seems to have an antipathy toward the soul, Godliness, and spirituality. It seems to be lying down under a burden, for it resists doing the *mitzvot* [commandments] of the Torah and responding to your higher thoughts. You, looking from your lofty "spiritual" perspective, might not want to help it. You might think that we should adopt fasts and self-mortifications to crush the body and break it. But no, says the Baal Shem, that is not the way to cause the light of Torah to enter. "You must surely help him," means that you must purify and refine the body, letting the soul's light shine through it.

—*from a retelling by Rabbi M. M. Schneerson in* Likutei Sichot *(1992)*[3]

becomes a clear, transparent expression of the soul. Body, mind, and soul are interactive and interdependent forces or vital energies. Each has its own purpose and contribution to our lives. No approach to health and fitness can succeed which does not take into account the complexity of our being in this world.

In short, our approach to physical health must involve the spirit, and our approach to spiritual growth must address the body. "Thin thighs in thirty days," diets, plastic surgery, barbells and bench presses, spas and surgeries—all these derive from a perspective alienated from the physical body, and all ultimately fail to promote true health. The body must be viewed as a teacher, a friend, and an essential guide, not to be abused and insulted by outside fixes.

At the same time, spiritual efforts must include loving attention to the physical body. The Torah tells us, "take the utmost care of your vital soul" (Deuteronomy 4:9), from which we learn that care for the body is a *mitzvah*, that is, a specific commandment from God.[4] Working with the body in a caring way will bring us closer to our true work on earth, to refine mind, body, and soul for ourselves, our families, our communities, and God.

When we do this, we have the possibility of experiencing ourselves, in our physical body, as souls. Rabbi Nachman of Breslov, one of the great Hasidic masters who delved into the mysteries of the body, taught that we need to attend to our body to open it to higher perceptions:

> For it is necessary to show great compassion for the body, to see to purifying it, so as to be able to inform it of all the insights and perceptions which the soul perceives. This is because the soul of every human being is continuously seeing and comprehending very exalted things. But the body knows nothing of them. Therefore, every person...should see to purifying the body so that the soul will be able to inform it of all that she is always seeing and comprehending.

This corresponds to: "From my flesh I will behold God" (Job 19.26)—specifically "my flesh." That is, the person—with his body—will see and behold exalted perceptions; that which the soul is always perceiving.[5]

☐ The Method

By working with the body in a spiritual mode, we can create a vessel for experiencing in this world what the soul experiences. Such an exalted goal may seem distant, but once we begin to work with our bodies from this new perspective, it begins to seem more possible.

Our approach must involve a discipline to continually remind ourselves that we are body, mind and soul, and to work on the ways we use our energy. Jewish tradition, with its positive view of the body and the physical world, offers rich resources grounded in the discipline of prayer. We focus on a few simple traditional prayers that anyone can learn, from the *Bircat Ha-Shachar* (Morning Blessings) found in the *siddur* (Jewish prayerbook). To accompany these we have developed themes from Jewish mysticism into meditations and movements to enrich our practice.

☐ Mind Work

By grounding ourselves in tradition, we can soar. The soaring comes in the discovery that prayer is not only a verbal process but a movement of the whole being. We open ourselves to this discovery when we learn how to imagine our bodies in ways that will help us connect to the prayers. Jewish mysticism helps in this process by providing some "maps" of the soul that can help us focus on energy centers of the body, places where our vitality is readily accessible and easily stimulated. With this wisdom, we can imprint on our physical, emotional, and mental bodies the higher realities of our being, and replace a mechanistic, alienated experience of our bodies with a holistic one.

In each of the following chapters, we will introduce a prayer, explore its meaning, and suggest exercises and meditations to help integrate the words and ideas with the body.

The explanations of the prayers are intended to help the mind connect with the words in our normal, cognitive mode.

☐ Body Work

The actual practice of the prayers comes at the end of each chapter, where the prayers are given in Hebrew, in transliteration, and in English. The exercises incorporate gentle and natural range-of-motion movements that will help you stretch and relax different areas of the body. They are not intended to be strenuous. If you experience pain or unusual tension when doing them, investigate the cause.

If you feel uncomfortable or ungraceful with the movements, don't be surprised—and don't give up. Movement with prayer is an unfamiliar experience for most of us who have been trained in a highly verbal and intellectual tradition. Keep practicing them on a daily basis until they feel familiar. Later, you may want to alter them as you come to understand the prayers more deeply.

If it is physically impossible for you to perform certain movements, do those that are possible for you; then visualize yourself doing the rest or improvise your own substitutes. While we have found these particular sets of movements very helpful, they are not the only possible ways to move with the prayers.

□ Return to the Soul

The meditations will imprint positive, beautiful, and harmonious thoughts, together with spiritual concepts, into your self-image. The images we carry in our minds are probably the most potent unconscious influences on our feelings and actions. When we learn to choose appropriate images, we offer ourselves not just a temporary injection of "positive thinking" but a rich mental picture of a spiritual approach to life. We also suggest sounds and sensations, which may be helpful to those who do not easily retain visual images.[6]

Such healthy images do for our minds what healthy food does for our bodies. This approach is implicit in Judaism's daily prayer service, which includes an entire section of praise to God, the *Pesuke d'Zimra* or "verses of song," that are full of rich imagery. In the standard service, these prepare us for the major prayers by directing our minds to positive images of God's relation to the world, in thanksgiving and praise.

The meditations and movements also offer an opportunity to familiarize ourselves with the energy centers in the body. These are represented in the system known as the *sefirot*. They are areas identified by the Jewish mysticism as fundamental to balancing body, mind, and soul. Attention is itself a positive act, and focusing on these energy centers is a first step in healing.

□ How to Proceed

Of course, the key to changing one's approach to health *or* to spiritual matters is the willingness to devote time to it. Moreover, the more clearly focused and the more receptive one's mind is during the time one sets aside, the more effective one's efforts will be. Generally, this means attending to prayer and exercise in the morning, when our minds are relatively clear and we are not yet involved in the day's activities. We suggest that you practice saying *Modeh Ani* first thing every morning, before your feet even hit the floor. Then do the first exercise, at the end of Chapter 1. After a few days, add the prayer in Chapter 2, together with its movements and meditation. Gradually, add the prayers, movements, and meditations from each chapter. Once you become familiar with these, the whole series will take only about 15 or 20 minutes. The Prayer Wheel at the front of the book summarizes the series for quick reference. Then, the Walking Meditation which is described after Chapter 6 is a good way to end your morning exercises.

Second, we recommend doing a longer meditation as often as possible—preferably two or three times a week. Choose from the Flowing Energy, Heart, Lower Waters, Temple of the Soul, Angelic Clouds, and Gift Meditations. An audiotape of these meditations is available from the publisher if you find it distracting to read while meditating. At night, you can reflect for a few minutes on your day and write briefly in a Journal of the *Sefirot*, described in Chapter 5. This is a structured way of looking at how each area of your life is developing, based on the Jewish mystical teachings about the soul's purpose, which we discuss in Chapter 6. In this way, you will gradually integrate more of your whole self into the prayer experience, so that the form of speech called "prayer" fully connects body, mind, and soul.

☐ Results: When You Align Body, Mind, and Soul

The more you commit to these prayers, exercises, and meditations over time, the greater the changes you will see in yourself. Your hunger for external satisfaction will diminish. You will want to exercise more, eat healthy foods, and open your mind to spiritual learning. The only "hunger" that increases is your yearning for deeper spirituality. Emotionally, you will want to overcome old obstacles and clear your heart of the familiar and repetitive blocks to healthy relationships. Emptiness, anger, fear, and boredom may still occur, but they will become doorways to richer experience of your inner self. The courage to feel such emotions can lead you to walk with God instead of escaping into consumerism, television, addictive substances, or senseless partying. You will be able to feel your natural heartbeat, or the presence of God. You will be ready to hear, with new clarity, *Shema Israel, Adonai Elohenu,*

Adonai Echad ("Hear O Israel, the Lord is our God, the Lord is One").

You will, in short, become transparent to your soul. Our bodies were created for this. As the Hasidic masters teach us, the ultimate purpose of Godliness is to become manifest in the physical.[7] This is the potential hidden within all our spiritual efforts, a potential that can become manifest when we work consciously with body, mind, and soul.

מוֹדֶה אֲנִי לְפָנֶיךָ, מֶלֶךְ חַי וְקַיָּם, שֶׁהֶחֱזַרְתָּ
בִּי נִשְׁמָתִי בְּחֶמְלָה. רַבָּה אֱמוּנָתֶךָ.

I thank You, O King who lives now and forever, that You have
restored to me my soul with mercy; great is Your faithfulness!

To practice the prayer with its movement and meditation, please turn to page 28.

1

Awakening

FOR CENTURIES, JEWS have awakened in the morning with this prayer on their lips. Children learn it before any other prayer. With these few words, said while we are still in bed, we express our awareness that soul and body are united, and that God has given us a gift of another day to fulfill our mission on earth.

Left to itself, the body would probably stay in bed a few more hours, if not forever. The body is dense energy, clinging to the earth. Gravity pulls it down. During sleep, the energy is quieted and compressed further. You can probably remember mornings when your limbs felt so heavy they seemed glued into the mattress. The soul, on the other hand, has the potential to detach from the body. So the first thing we do, before we even get out of bed, is to acknowledge our gratitude for the life-force we feel within us.

The relation between the body *(guf)* and soul or spirit (which the Hebrew Bible variously refers to as *nefesh, ruach,* or *neshamah*) is very intimate. Some of our Jewish sages have described them as "married": Like a husband and wife, body and soul are independent actors, but they are so intimately interrelated that one cannot be touched without affecting the other.

As the *Code of Jewish Law* explains, "when a person is asleep, the holy soul departs from his body."[1] Body and soul go to their separate domains during sleep; upon awakening, they are fully united again. A new day is like a wedding, with your blanket as the *chupah* or marriage canopy. So take a moment each morning to celebrate the joy of this reunion, and sing *Modeh Ani*, "I give thanks."

This prayer also prepares us to move beyond our egos and awaken our spiritual selves. Each day, our awareness of individuality, of "I," emerges as we awaken. With the *Modeh Ani*, we begin to consecrate this "I" to God.

This is what it means to say a prayer first thing in the morning. As the Torah teaches, we are to bring the "first and best" to God. In the days of the Temple, Jews brought the first-born of each of their domestic animals as offerings. They tied a ribbon around the first-budding fruit on their fruit trees to mark the offering to be brought as "first fruits." The first-born son was consecrated to the priesthood, so it was necessary to redeem or "buy him back" from the *cohanim* (priests)—a ceremony still practiced symbolically today. All these offerings remind us that the Jewish people are a holy priesthood—"a kingdom of *cohanim*" as the Torah says, designated for service.[2] This service begins immediately when we wake, so that we consecrate the moment of our first awareness to God.

Then, like the *cohanim* before daily service, we rinse our hands, eyes, and mouth, and we say the blessing over washing hands:

בָּרוּךְ אַתָּה, יהוה, אֱלֹהֵינוּ מֶלֶךְ הָעוֹלָם, אֲשֶׁר קִדְּשָׁנוּ בְּמִצְוֹתָיו, וְצִוָּנוּ עַל נְטִילַת יָדַיִם.

Bar-ruch a-ta, A-do-nai, El-o-he-nu me-lech ha-o-lam, a-sher kid'sha-nu b'mitz-vo-tav v'tzi-va-nu al n'ti-lat ya-da-yim.

Blessed are You, Adonai, Our God, Ruler of the universe, who sanctified us with commandments and commanded us to raise [wash] our hands.

With this preparation for the service of our daily lives, we begin to create a spiritual intention, the intention that body and soul should work together.

Most couples are not perfectly matched, of course, and neither are body and soul. The body is dense and involved in its own processes. The soul is light and airy, yearning for realms beyond. Our job is to help the body receive the soul, and to keep the soul focused on its work in this world. The challenge is to be fully aware of both.

The breath is one of God's gifts that helps make the connection between body and soul, like a thread that sews them together. God "breathed the soul" into Adam, the first human being (Genesis 2:7), and the breath is a constant and crucial element in spiritual awareness. Using the breath, we can awaken the body, helping ourselves to become aware of the soul's presence. The breath is the pathfinder for the soul.

Breath is purifying as well. Just as we wash with water on the outside, the moist, warm breath cleanses the inside. Try it: Breathe deeply and with joy.

The whole body can be opened and cleansed through a simple physical warm-up, with attention to the breath. Here it is:

First, think of your body as being divided into three regions: the intellectual, the emotional, and the physical body. The intellectual centers in the head and neck, the emotional in the upper torso and arms, the physical in the lower torso, extending down to the feet which represent action in the world. As we will see later, these correspond to three areas marked out by the Kabbalistic system of *sefirot*, the "map of the soul" in Jewish tradition (see p. 54).

Now try the exercises. You will perform each movement within the natural range of motion of your joints, without straining. Do it as completely as you can, but do not cause yourself pain. If you are physically unable to do any part of a movement, close your eyes and imagine yourself doing it.

You will then do the same exercise again, with deeper breathing. Don't worry about whether you should breathe "in" or "out" on a certain schedule. Just breathe the way that comes naturally to you, trusting your own body and thinking of the breath as a fresh sea breeze that cleanses every part of your body. The initial movement, followed by doing it with deeper, more conscious breathing, is a way to weave the "breath" of the soul into the body.

After each set of exercises, visualize the "soul map" that corresponds to that area of the body, and breathe into the points of energy as they are described. You will soon become more familiar with these, as we return to them in other sections of the book.

The exercises may seem simple, but you will be surprised how, when repeated daily, they increase your awareness of your body as a potential vessel for Divine light.

Opening to the Light:
Movement and Meditations for *Modeh Ani*

מוֹדֶה אֲנִי לְפָנֶיךָ, מֶלֶךְ חַי וְקַיָּם, שֶׁהֶחֱזַרְתָּ
בִּי נִשְׁמָתִי בְּחֶמְלָה. רַבָּה אֱמוּנָתֶךָ.

*Mo-deh a-ni l'fa-ne-cha, me-lech chai v'ka-yam, she-he-che-zar-ta bi
nish-ma-ti b'chem-la, rab-ba e-mu-na-te-cha.*

I thank You, O King who lives now and forever, that You have restored to me my soul with mercy; great is Your faithfulness!

Wash your hands in the following way: Fill with water a large cup that has a smooth rim. Take the cup in the right hand, transfer it to the left, and pour some of the water over the right wrist and hand; then switch hands and pour over the left. Repeat two more times on each hand for a total of six pourings. Then say the blessing:

בָּרוּךְ אַתָּה, יהוה, אֱלֹהֵינוּ מֶלֶךְ הָעוֹלָם, אֲשֶׁר
קִדְּשָׁנוּ בְּמִצְוֹתָיו, וְצִוָּנוּ עַל נְטִילַת יָדָיִם.

*Ba-ruch a-ta, Ado-nai, El-o-he-nu Me-lech ha-o-lam, a-sher kid'sha-
nu b'mitz-vo-tav v'tzi-va-nu al ne-ti-lat ya-da-yim.*

Blessed are You, Adonai, Our God, Ruler of the universe, who sanctified us with commandments and commanded us to raise [wash] our hands.

Now do the following exercise:

First, make sure you have a good, firm stance: Stand with your feet apart, at shoulder width. Your knees should be slightly bent and your pelvis tipped slightly forward so that your buttocks are tucked under you. This is your basic starting body position throughout this exercise.

Deep breathing is important here. We suggest where to inhale and exhale, but the main point is to breathe naturally and deeply. If it is difficult to pay attention to the breathing instructions, just remember that an upward movement is accompanied by an inhale, and a downward movement by an exhale. Breathing is like an up-and-down wave.

As you raise both arms from the sides of your body over your head, breathe in deeply. As you lower your arms, breathe out. Your head will naturally tip up and then return to a normal position. Do this three times.

HEAD AND NECK

Purpose: To awaken the brain functions (the intellectual body) and clear the sense organs for sight, hearing, smell and taste.

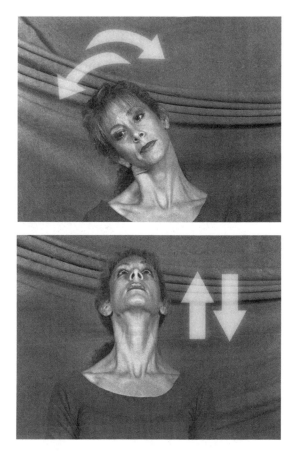

Instructions:

1. Standing in the same position, breathe in, and tip your right ear as far as you comfortably can toward your right shoulder. Leave it there as you breathe out slowly. Repeat with left ear to left shoulder. Do this three times, breathing deeply with the movement.

2. Nod your chin toward your chest, then look up slightly. (Don't stretch the neck backward.) Exhale as your head goes forward, inhale as it returns to the upright position. Repeat two more times, adding a deep, natural breath.

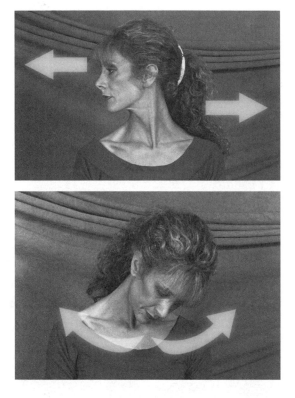

3. Look over your right shoulder, then your left. Repeat twice more, breathing in and out with the movement.

4. Breathe in. Gently roll your chin from the right side toward the left, letting your chin sink toward your chest in the center while exhaling. Return to the other side. (Roll *only* frontward.) The movement is like drawing a smile with your nose. Repeat twice more with deep breathing.

Pause for a brief meditation.

Imagine small golden circles appearing around your head, one at your right temple, one at your left temple, and one at your throat. Together they mark a triangle. With your head comfortably in an upright position, inhale and exhale three times, once for each circle. With each breath, imagine a stream of golden light entering the top of your head and filling the triangle with golden light. Exhale any confusion or murkiness. The golden light begins to vibrate and radiate, awakening your sleeping mind. Any extraneous thoughts or worries dissolve. Your mind becomes clear and open so that you can receive the light, the new intelligence and guidance that God has in store for you today.

UPPER TORSO

Purpose: To open the lungs and chest for full breathing; and to open the heart to other people and to the world.

Shoulder and Arm Rolls:

1. Standing in the same position, you will try to isolate only the upper body. Roll your shoulders up, back and down in a circular motion. Breathe in as the shoulders come up, out as they roll down. Do this three times, then reverse direction and circle three times. Lift your shoulders up and down three times, as if shrugging them. Inhale as you lift them,

exhale as you release. Accompany each roll and shrug with deep breathing.

2. Put your left hand on your waist. Tilt your upper body slightly to the left and reach out with your right arm. Move your right shoulder and right arm in a wide circle, as if washing a huge picture window. As you reach forward and to the left, breathe in; as you move to the right and back, breathe out. Repeat three times, breathing deeply and imagining your entire right side opening up to the fresh air. Then repeat with your left arm.

3. Reach your right arm back and circle the entire arm and shoulder up, over, and forward, as if throwing a ball. Breathe in as you reach back, and out as you circle forward and down. Do this with your right arm and shoulder three times, breathing deeply. Repeat with your left arm and shoulder.

Rib Cage:

Extend both arms out to the sides. Breathe in. Reach alternately to the far right and left sides without turning your torso, like a typewriter carriage shifting from right to left and back again. Exhale as you reach and stretch, inhale as you return to upright position. Repeat twice more.

Upper Back and Chest Stretch:

1. Extend your arms forward. Lace your fingers together and turn your palms outward. Take a deep breath. Then stretch your arms, pushing your palms forward so that the area between your shoulder blades widens. Exhale, stretching your upper back. Make sure your hips are pressed forward. Your upper torso and hips will seem to be curled around a large ball in a C-shape. Hold for a count of eight, breathing in and out, then relax. Repeat.

2. Reach behind your body and interlace the fingers of your hands (palms toward the body), squeezing your shoulder blades together. Breathe in, raise your chest and stretch, opening the heart space as you breathe deeply. Exhale and hold for a count of eight, breathing in and out if you need to. Relax. Now repeat with deep breathing.

Pause for a brief meditation.

Imagine three silver balls outlining your upper torso, one at your right shoulder, another at your left shoulder, and one at the place of your heart. Imagine that the three points are connected so they form a triangular cup. Now a stream of silver light comes down from above, directly into the heart. Inhale deeply, and let the light fill the triangular cup that is bringing energy to your chest region and enlivening your heart and your emotions. As you exhale, breathe out any darkness, any emotional pain, sorrow, or sadness. Inhale and exhale three times. Your chest now radiates silver light, and your heart awakens with each breath and opens like a beautiful Torah scroll. Your heart is open to receive God's love and to give God's love. You now feel new strength to cope, and you are protected by love. Your emotions are balanced and pure. You feel the heart completely open now, filled with love and compassion.

LOWER TORSO AND PELVIS

Purpose: To open all the vessels for cleaning and purifying our bodies, and to align our passions and animal instincts with God.

Instructions:

1. With feet shoulder-width apart, firmly planted into the floor, and knees relaxed, rock your hips gently forward and back three times. Breathe in as your hips rock forward, out as they rock back.

2. Squeeze the buttocks tightly three times to awaken the muscles that support the base of the spine and lower back. Breathe naturally. Repeat another three squeezes.

3. Breathing deeply and naturally, circle your hips around to the left in an easy circle, three times, then circle to the right three times. Repeat.

Pause for a brief meditation.

Imagine three copper-colored balls outlining your lower torso, one at the right hip, one at the left, one at the pubic bone. They connect to form a triangle. Imagine a stream of copper light coming from above directly into your pelvis, filling this triangular cup. This area represents your instinctual physical body. Inhale deeply three times. As you exhale, breathe out any darkness, discomfort or fatigue, and any physical ailments that stand in your way. As the copper light becomes brighter, feel the physical body take on new strength, free of anything that is not for your highest good.

Your physical body is now connected to a higher source. Your hips are ready to provide you with stability and steadiness through your day. Any healing you need in your physical body is generated by this strong new light.

LEGS AND FEET

Purpose: To bring fresh energy to the muscles which give us support in the world, and to help us walk with integrity, following God's pathway for us.

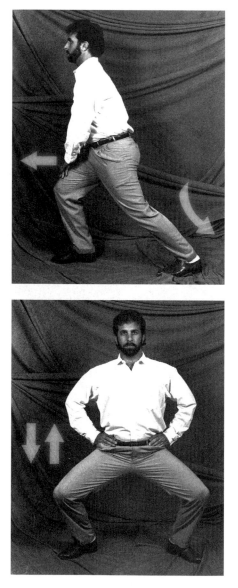

Instructions:

1. Lunges: Separate the feet a little wider. Turn toward the right and bend your right knee, straightening the left leg and leaning forward to make a gentle "lunge" to the right. Exhale. Your feet do not have to be in a straight line; they may be shoulder width apart to maintain your balance. Breathe in and gently straighten your back leg more, by pushing the heel of your back leg to the floor, stretching the hamstring muscles. Exhale. Hold the position for eight counts as you breathe in and out naturally. Straighten up gently, then repeat.

Turn to the center and breathe deeply two times. Then turn to the left and repeat the lunge, gently stretching the hamstring of the right leg. Straighten, then repeat. Return to center.

2. Knee Bends: With your legs spread at hip width and toes turned slightly out, squeeze the buttocks tightly. Keep them tight, as this stabilizes the lower back and pelvis and helps strengthen the lower abdominals. Breathe in, then bend your knees slightly as you exhale. Keep your knees over your toes as you bend. Then straighten the legs and return to upright position. You may want to try shifting your weight to the outsides of the feet to feel more of the buttocks and back of the leg. Repeat three times. Stand in upright position and relax, gently shaking either leg if your knees feel tight. Then repeat with attention to your breathing. Always keep pelvis underneath you—don't arch your back.

3. Toe Raises: With legs spread comfortably, raise yourself on your toes and inhale, letting your weight rest on the first two toes of each foot. You will be leaning forward very slightly. Hold for a moment, then return your heels to the floor as you exhale. Repeat three times.

Pause for a brief meditation:

Imagine that the golden cup of light in your head now extends downward through your body, into a circle between the feet. The silver light from the chest and the copper from the pelvis join the gold, and the streams of light become a triangle, with its corners at the two knees and the feet—the last triangular cup.

Inhale and exhale three times. Begin to feel a warm glow in your feet. Know that as you walk today, your footsteps are guided by the alignment of your mind, body, and soul, resonating with the walk of God.

Throughout your day, know that you have a unique mission and a purpose in life. Each time you remember your connection to the energy of the light, it will be a source of faith and trust, strength and purpose for you.

מַה-טֹּבוּ אֹהָלֶיךָ, יַעֲקֹב, מִשְׁכְּנֹתֶיךָ, יִשְׂרָאֵל. וַאֲנִי, בְּרֹב
חַסְדְּךָ אָבֹא בֵיתֶךָ, אֶשְׁתַּחֲוֶה אֶל-הֵיכַל קָדְשְׁךָ בְּיִרְאָתֶךָ.
יהוה, אָהַבְתִּי מְעוֹן בֵּיתֶךָ, וּמְקוֹם מִשְׁכַּן כְּבוֹדֶךָ. וַאֲנִי
אֶשְׁתַּחֲוֶה וְאֶכְרָעָה, אֶבְרְכָה לִפְנֵי-יהוה עֹשִׂי. וַאֲנִי תְפִלָּתִי
לְךָ, יהוה, עֵת רָצוֹן. אֱלֹהִים, בְּרָב-חַסְדֶּךָ, עֲנֵנִי בֶּאֱמֶת יִשְׁעֶךָ.

How fair are your tents, O Jacob, and your dwelling places, O Israel!
As for me, through Your abundant kindness I will enter Your house;
I will prostrate myself toward Your Holy Sanctuary in awe of You.
Adonai, I love Your house and the dwelling place of Your Glory.
I will prostrate myself and bow, kneeling before Adonai my Maker.
As for me, may my prayer to You be at a pleasing time.
God, in Your abundant kindness, answer me with the truth of Your
salvation.[1]

To practice the prayer with its movement and meditation, please turn to page 41.

2
Entering
Sacred
Space

WITH THE *MODEH ANI,* we acknowledge that we are spiritual beings. We refresh and remind ourselves of our service by a ritual washing. We open ourselves to the purifying breath of life, and the refining influence of our own soul. Now we are ready to meet with God.

The Sages tell us that it is important to have a place where we talk to God. We need a "temple," a miniature *Mishkan* or "dwelling place" for the divine. We may be entering the synagogue, or we may be in the privacy of our own homes. In either case, we create our space with one of the morning prayers, known as the *Mah Tovu.*

Surprisingly, the first line of this beautiful and touching song was first uttered by an enemy of the Jewish people! The king of Moab had hired a certain Balaam as a sorcerer to curse the Jews. But, because Balaam was a true prophet, he could utter only the words that God gave him. Against his will, God turned his curses into blessings (see Numbers

23:1-24:25). To Balaam's utterance have been added verses from various psalms.

Mah to-vu o-ha-le-cha... "How fair are your tents!" The "tents" are houses of study and prayer. In those times, they were truly tents—private tents for each family, and the *Mishkan* or holy tabernacle. The midrash says that Balaam, looking down from a cliff on the encampment of the Children of Israel, noticed how carefully the people placed their tents so that one could not look into a neighbor's tent.[2] He was impressed at how the Israelites respected one another's privacy. The Sages later extolled this *tzniut,* or modesty, as one of the distinguishing characteristics of the Jewish people.

The most famous of tents was the tent of *Sarah Imenu,* Sarah our mother, the wife of Abraham. Rashi,[3] the great biblical commentator of the eleventh century, tells us that when Abraham came to where they first settled in the land of Israel, he set up Sarah's tent first, because she was a greater prophet than he. Sarah taught the women, and Abraham taught the men. Sarah's holiness was so great, the midrash says, that her bread stayed fresh from week to week, her Shabbat lights burned until the next Friday night, and a Divine Cloud hovered over her tent. These were the same miracles that occurred later in the *Mishkan* in the desert and the *Beit HaMikdash* or Holy Temple in Jerusalem. These descriptions express symbolically the idea that a holy person, or a place of holy ceremony, can bring down extraordinary blessings on the physical, mental, and spiritual levels.

We can make our own home a "tent" for the worship of God and the study of Torah. Likewise, we can experience the body with its aura as the movable "tent" for our soul. As Rabbi Matityahu Glazerson observes, the Jewish mystical tradition regards the energy field around us as our "tent" where we can come close to God.[4] It is a place where God's glory resides. We can enter it simply by giving it our attention, anywhere and anytime, since God's Light is present everywhere and all the time.[5]

According to Jewish mysticism, the body corresponds to the *Mishkan,* the portable temple where the Israelites worshipped in the wilderness. Our bodies can be a dwelling-place for God just as the *Mishkan* was. The heart and mind in the upper part of the body correspond to the Holy of Holies in the *Mishkan,* while the stomach and lower parts of the body, the area of integration and refinement, correspond to the area known as the Holy. These vital inner organs are framed by the skeleton and muscles, covered with flesh just as the beams of the *Mishkan* were covered with gold. Our primary sense organs are represented by the menorah, with its seven branches corresponding to the seven "lights" in the face—two eyes, ears, and nostrils, and one mouth.[6] We relate to the outer world through our hands and feet. Their service and action correspond to the sacrifices on the outer altar and symbolize that every action, even in the outside world, is a gift we want to give to God.

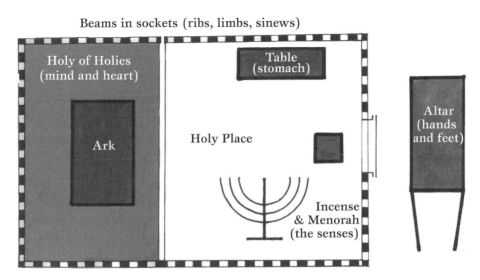

Beams in sockets (ribs, limbs, sinews)

Holy of Holies (mind and heart)

Table (stomach)

Altar (hands and feet)

Ark

Holy Place

Incense & Menorah (the senses)

The *Mishkan* or "Tabernacle"

You find in the *Mishkan* that the beams were fixed into the sockets,
    and in the body the ribs are fixed into the vertebrae,....
In the *Mishkan* the beams were covered with gold,
    in the body the ribs are covered with flesh,....
In the *Mishkan* there were bolts in the beams to keep them upright,
    and in the body limbs and sinews are drawn to keep man upright,....
In the *Mishkan* the veil divided between the Holy-place and the Holy-of-Holies,
    and in the body the diaphragm divides the heart from the stomach...

—*Midrash* Bereishit Rabba[7]

B'rov chas-de-cha, "Through your abundant kindness," begins the second verse of our prayer. God's *chesed* or lovingkindness is pervasive, protecting us at all times. The "tent" can protect us from negative people, especially from their anger. A phrase found in many of our prayers is *ki l'olam chasdo,* "for your lovingkindness is forever." We can experience that constant presence whenever we turn our attention to the aura around our bodies, the spiritual tent that God provides.

A-vo vei-te-cha, "I will enter *Your* house." This can have a dual meaning. First, we are invited into God's house and accepted with unconditional love. Like the pure love of a child, who is simply glad to see us, God's love is welcoming. Second, when we recognize that God has made our bodies a "house" for the Divine, we are filled with love, awe and reverence in return.

A-ni esh-ta-cha-veh v'ech-ra-ah e-vr'cha, "I will prostrate myself and bow and kneel." This phrase acknowledges the sense of awe that sometimes comes over us when we contemplate God. Seeing a cantor bend in devotion, bowing toward the ark, or prostrating ourselves completely on Yom Kippur can evoke that sense of awe. We can also call to mind Isaac, the son of Abraham, who was so complete in his love and reverence for God that even when he was about to be sacrificed on the altar, he never protested. In our private prayer, we can imagine a wondrous beam of light connecting us to God. As we bow, we shower light around us.

Va-ani, t'fi-la-ti l'cha A-do-nai et ra-tzon, "As for me, may my prayer to You, Adonai, be at a pleasing time." Customarily, this means the time when others are praying in the synagogue, even if we are in our private homes. The deeper reason is that Jewish life operates on a different temporal scheme than the linear time of everyday life. We live in circular or spiral time where each Shabbat, each holiday, and each segment of the day has its own identity, mood and feeling, like a separate territory with its own climate. Every Passover, we enter the same time-territory where Passover was celebrated in Egypt, and where Joshua's armies celebrated it upon entering Israel—the same "space" where it has been celebrated for over 3,000 years, wherever Jews have lived. Every Yom Kippur we enter into the same time in which the Jews were forgiven for the sin of making the golden calf. Once we move into the eye of the holiday, we enter a kind of time-tunnel, where we can step into ancient shoes and see through more ancient eyes.

Likewise, every time we join with the time-territory of morning prayer, we enter the time when worship took place in the Jerusalem's Holy Temple, the time when the Jewish people always sing their prayers to God. The vibrations of sound never end, so the prayers and chants reverberate through time. For this reason, joining prayers with others is not merely a matter of numbers of people, but also a matter of the "pleasing time," a time when God and we have a desire to express our intimate relationship. Jacob, Isaac's son, reminds us of the mystery of time because he was promised that God would protect him from the *time* he left Israel until his return (Genesis 28:15). The span of time turned out to be 22 years. Likewise, he agreed to work for seven years to marry Rachel, but the years seemed to him but a few days (Genesis 29:20). Jacob's patience, faith, and confidence in being protected can inspire us to develop the trust that allows us to take the time for prayer, and experience each moment as a gift from God.

These thoughts are threads that can attune our minds and emotions to spiritual things, enabling us to weave a garment for our divine soul. We can complete this enclothing through body movements that re-create Sarah's or Abraham's tent and build our personal *mishkan* in which it is easier to open ourselves to the influence of the soul, easier to let ourselves come close to God.

Here is a gentle exercise and meditation that can help create this energy. We suggest you say the prayer aloud, then perform the movements while repeating the words silently to yourself. Follow these with the short meditation.

Creating Sarah's Tent

Following is the *Mah Tovu* in Hebrew text, transliteration, and English translation. At the beginning, you may want to say the prayers first and then do the movements, because each may be unfamiliar. As you become more comfortable with them, you can integrate the movements into each line of the prayer. You will find your own tempo for saying the prayer and doing the movements, until they eventually flow together. With these exercises, you need not be concerned about breathing, as you will be occupied in saying the prayers.

מַה-טֹּבוּ אֹהָלֶיךָ, יַעֲקֹב, מִשְׁכְּנֹתֶיךָ, יִשְׂרָאֵל. וַאֲנִי, בְּרֹב
חַסְדְּךָ אָבֹא בֵיתֶךָ, אֶשְׁתַּחֲוֶה אֶל-הֵיכַל קָדְשְׁךָ בְּיִרְאָתֶךָ.
יהוה, אָהַבְתִּי מְעוֹן בֵּיתֶךָ, וּמְקוֹם מִשְׁכַּן כְּבוֹדֶךָ. וַאֲנִי
אֶשְׁתַּחֲוֶה וְאֶכְרָעָה, אֶבְרְכָה לִפְנֵי-יהוה עֹשִׂי. וַאֲנִי תְפִלָּתִי
לְךָ, יהוה, עֵת רָצוֹן. אֱלֹהִים, בְּרָב-חַסְדֶּךָ, עֲנֵנִי בֶּאֱמֶת יִשְׁעֶךָ.

Mah to-vu o-ha-le-cha, Ya-a-kov, mish-ke-no-te-cha, Yis-ra-el.
Va-ani, b'rov chas-de-cha, a-vo vei-te-cha, esh-ta-cha-veh el hei-chal
kad-she-cha b'yira-te-cha. A-do-nai, a-hav-ti m'on bei-te-cha, u-ma-
kom mish-kan k'vo-de-cha. Va-a-ni esh-ta-cha-veh v'ech-ra-ah, e-
vr'cha lif-nei A-do-nai o-si. Va-a-ni, t'fi-la-ti l'cha A-do-nai et ra-tzon,
El-o-him b'rav chas-de-cha, a-ne-ni be-emet yi-she-cha.

How fair are your tents, O Jacob, and your dwelling places,
   O Israel!
As for me, through Your abundant kindness I will enter
   Your house;
I will prostrate myself toward Your Holy Sanctuary in awe
   of You.
Adonai, I love Your house and the dwelling-place of Your Glory.
I will prostrate myself and bow, kneeling before Adonai
   my Maker.
As for me, may my prayer to You be at a pleasing time.
God, in Your abundant kindness, answer me with the truth of
   Your salvation.

You can stand or sit for this exercise.

"How fair are your tents, O Jacob, and your dwelling places, O Israel!"
This line of the prayer is said slowly, accompanying the movements of
"drawing" the shape of the tent.

"How fair..."

1. Before you begin, focus on the strong intent we need in our arms.
They will be your "paintbrushes" drawing the energy around you.
Extend them straight out and feel their strength, but without locking

them rigidly. Your fingers also point straight out from the line of the arm, as if they are sending out energy.

2. First, draw the sides of the tent as follows: Turn your upper body toward the right, twisting as far back as you can without straining, and extending your right arm behind you at the height of your chest. Turn your body slowly back toward the front, using your taut arm to draw a half circle in the air beside you. End with the right arm pointing directly to the front, still at chest height.

With the right arm still extended, turn your upper body to the left, extending your left arm behind you at the height of your chest, reaching back as far as is comfortable. Turn back to the front, drawing a half circle through the air on the left, ending with your left arm in front, parallel to your right arm.

"...are your tents, O Jacob..."

3. Both arms are extended in front of the chest. Now you are ready to draw the roof. Raise your arms together, reaching straight up over your head. Hold them there while you look up and "see" the top of your tent. Bring your arms down to your sides, keeping them straight and ending with your fingers pointing toward the floor.

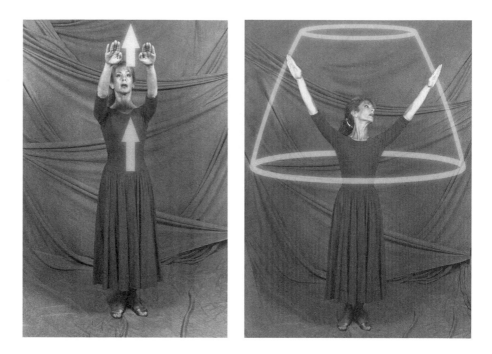

"...and your dwelling places, O Israel!"

4. Now you will draw the floor of the tent. Turn your upper body to the right as you did when drawing the sides in step two, but this time your right arm is down, fingers pointing toward the floor. Reach back as far as you can, then slowly turn to the front and draw a half circle around you. End with your right arm in front of you, pointing at a spot

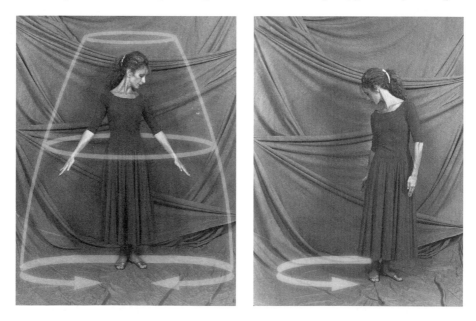

about one foot in front of your toes. Repeat the same movements on the left side, turning to the back, slowly turning forward while your fingers draw a half circle, and ending with your left arm in front, parallel to your right arm.

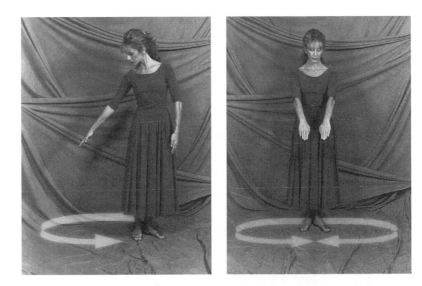

"As for me, through Your abundant kindness I will enter Your house; I will prostrate myself toward Your Holy Sanctuary in awe of You."

5. Raise your arms above your head again and look up, imagining an awesome shower of golden light, flowing in through your hands and your heart, filling you with love and acceptance. Hold this position to the end of this section of the prayer.

"Adonai, I love Your house and the dwelling-place of Your Glory."

6. Place your left hand over your heart, then cover it with your right hand. Become aware of the warmth of your hands.

"I will prostrate myself and bow, kneeling before Adonai my Maker."

7. Bow deeply, still holding your heart with both hands, in humble acceptance of the love of God.

"As for me, may my prayer to You be at a pleasing time. God, in Your abundant kindness, answer me with the truth of Your salvation."

Open your hands, stretch your arms forward, and turn the palms upward to receive God's light with your hands. Tilt your head up slightly as you once again imagine the light shining in through the top of the tent.

Meditation

Take a deep breath and close your eyes. See Sarah's tent, surrounding you. See the beauty of this sacred space that is yours and God's. You have prepared your house, as if for a special and beloved guest, and it feels wonderful. Your Mishkan *can go anywhere with you.*

Lift your face slowly. Lift your chest slowly. Feel a shower of divine, unconditional love fill your heart. Feel yourself returning it with even more exuberance and passion. This is your relationship with God.

Finally, be aware of the power in the timing for making this connection with your community, with the Jewish people, with the grand design. Imagine the tents of each Jew in the world from all time, and imagine the thousands of tents that are opening this morning, like constellations in the heavens. You now have a bond with your Jewish community, past, present, and future.

בָּרוּךְ אַתָּה, יהוה, אֱלֹהֵינוּ מֶלֶךְ הָעוֹלָם, אֲשֶׁר יָצַר
אֶת-הָאָדָם בְּחָכְמָה, וּבָרָא בוֹ נְקָבִים נְקָבִים, חֲלוּלִים
חֲלוּלִים. גָּלוּי וְיָדוּעַ לִפְנֵי כִסֵּא כְבוֹדֶךָ, שֶׁאִם יִפָּתֵחַ אֶחָד
מֵהֶם, אוֹ יִסָּתֵם אֶחָד מֵהֶם, אִי אֶפְשָׁר לְהִתְקַיֵּם וְלַעֲמוֹד
לְפָנֶיךָ. בָּרוּךְ אַתָּה, יהוה, רוֹפֵא כָל-בָּשָׂר וּמַפְלִיא לַעֲשׂוֹת.

Blessed are You, Adonai our God, Ruler of the Universe, who has formed
the human being with wisdom, and has created in us a multitude of openings and cavities. It is obvious and known before Your glorious Throne
that if but one of these were open [that should be closed], or one were
closed [that should be open], we would be unable to stay alive and stand
before You. Blessed are You, Adonai who heals all flesh and does wonders!

To practice the prayer with its movement and meditation, please turn to page 71.

3

The
Gift
of
the
Body

OUR BODIES, with their incredible complexity, are gifts from God. This gift includes every tiny blood vessel and neural synapse as well as the large organs that control our basic life processes. We contemplate this miracle and thank our Creator each morning, and also after relieving ourselves, with the *Asher Yatzar* prayer.

This seems to be a simple prayer of thanks for the body. Hidden within it, however, are allusions to many layers of meaning embedded in the shape and structure of our bodies, the "multitude of openings" that are gates to understanding. We can appreciate the prayer more—and our bodies more—if we understand some of them.

We can begin with a basic explanation of the words, then analyze the body more deeply.

A-sher ya-tzar et ha-a-dam b'hokh-mah, "...Who has formed the human being with wisdom." In creating human beings, God gave them the gift of wisdom, not merely in the head but also in the intricacies of the bodily organs and all their functions. So much goes on in our bodies automatically, without being aware of it. If our body is efficient, whom do we thank? Usually we take that Power for granted. The concrete language of *asher yatzar* can remind us of a very tangible and intricate reality that is God's handiwork.

At the same time, the word for "wisdom" here is *chochmah*, the divine inspiration and seed which manifests in the world. We are created "in wisdom," and are asked to imagine our bodies as a flow of creative thought-energy, all stemming from God.

A-sher ya-tzar, "Who has formed..." The body is not merely a construction of chemical compounds but a work of art. Some translations of this prayer render *yatzar* as "formed," while others say it means "fashioned." In contemporary terms, "fashion" may better convey the meaning, since it suggests the state-of-the-art, the highest quality. *Yatzar* is the same word that is used to describe a potter forming a shape out of clay, again suggesting the artist at work. That is how we need to see the efficiency of the human body—not as a machine but as a dynamic play of forces or, to use a musical metaphor, a symphony of harmonies and rhythms.

Ni-ka-vim, ni-ka-vim, cha-lu-lim cha-lu-lim, "A multitude of openings and cavities," or, alternately, "many ducts and tubes." These include the openings that lead in and out of the body, and the inner hollows that contain the organs such as lungs, heart, intestines, and brain. This reference to the cavities which contain the organs reminds us that the body itself contains an allusion to the Torah: Its 248 "organs and limbs," and 365 "sinews," correspond to the 248 positive commandments and 365 negative commandments of the Torah. Similarly, Rabbi Tanhum in the Talmud asserted that the eighteen blessings of the *Shemoneh Esreh* (the standing prayer said at each weekday service) correspond to the eighteen vertebrae of the spine (*Berachot* 28b). The body's dependence on the harmony of its organs is like the dynamic dance of the Torah that provides the spiritual infrastructure of our lives.

As we more deeply appreciate the different regions and functions of our body, we also learn gratitude for its miraculous construction. In turn, we develop greater sensitivity to our own bodies. This was one of the purposes of the sacrifices that were brought to the *Beit HaMikdash* (Holy Temple) in Jerusalem. The animal being offered represented the sacrifice of the ego of the offerer. Yet it was not brought to the fire whole, but piece by piece. The offerers of the sacrifice were supposed to consider the various parts of their bodies, and whether and how they had used those parts in the service of God. When we express gratitude for our health, or concern for our physical bodies, we also can "take it apart" mentally, thanking God for a multitude of miracles in the creation of physical beings.

> ...Gratitude for one's body and life is not sufficiently fulfilled by expressing thanks for the entire body at once, but rather by considering each limb separately, and understanding the kindness of the Creator which each part of the body demonstrates.... One should spend time to consider the wondrous benefits of the head, of each arm and each leg, and of every part of the body: "All of my parts say: Hashem, who is like unto You?" (Tehillim 35.10) Each limb sings its own song of praise and gratitude to the Creator.
>
> —*Rabbi Avigdor Miller,* **A Kingdom of Cohanim** *(1994)*[1]

Lif-ne chi-say ch'vo-de-cha, "Before Your glorious throne." We stand as bodies, not disembodied spirits, before God. Even while surrounded by myriads of angelic beings singing praises, God is also concerned with the opening and closing of each tiny tube in the human body. Whether it is the openings that cleanse, or the senses that are the window and doors of the soul, or those that regenerate human life, every duct and tube is important. This tells us also that God is always aware of and concerned with the mundane needs of each individual.

Ro-feh chal ba-sar u-maf-li la-asot, "Who heals all flesh and does wonders." The delicate balance of our organs is a wonder of wonders, as is every act of healing. A soul's entry into the body is another miracle, and its purpose is to help heal the world through accomplishing its mission. Of course, not every person who gets sick is "healed" in the human sense, nor is every prayer answered by a miracle. God's knowledge of the ultimate healing of *all* flesh extends beyond the scope of any human life, into all the incarnations of every soul, and into the grand scheme of the healing of the whole world. What we can learn is how to turn to God to help heal our pain, in the midst of the frailties of human life.

Miriam's Well

Picturing ourselves as filled with ducts, tubes and openings is, at first glance, a little strange. What is it really about? To experience our bodies more deeply, we need to turn the microscope, so to speak, to another level of magnification. We will look at the energy flow of our bodies as well as the functions of our organs. We will also meditate on the body's energy centers—the places where energy is more focused and readily accessed—as they are understood in Judaism. This is expressed in the system generally known as the *sefirot*. But first, we need to expand our ideas about the body.

For most of us, our conception of human anatomy began when our parents and early teachers taught us about the organs of the body—heart, lungs, stomach, brain. Later, we learned to organize those into systems of increasing complexity: respiratory, digestive, circulatory, neural. These terms were useful, but not designed to promote healing thoughts. One could argue, in fact, that most of the early terms we learned were connected with pain: "Where does it hurt? Oh, that's your stomach."

To make this clear, we can think of our physical bodies as composed mostly of water, living and moving as a circulation of air and fluids. The constant circulation inside us of oxygen and carbon dioxide, blood, lymph, and electrical energy is much of what we mean when we refer to feeling our own vitality.

Classic Jewish sources understood the energy that passes through our nerves also as a liquid, though we call it electrical.[2] This too is "living water" within us. The life-giving fluids and the electrical vibrations of our bodies parallel, on the physical level, the Torah, which is the "living water" for our souls. They are an analogy for the "wisdom" that flows into our bodies: *asher yatzar et ha-adam b'chochmah*—"Who forms the human being with wisdom."

We can understand something of the spiritual meaning of the flowing energy of water through the biblical figure of the prophetess Miriam, Moses' sister. The Torah tells us that, while the Jewish people were wandering in the desert, water was scarce. Twice, in response to the people's complaints, God had Moses bring water out of a rock for them (Exodus 17:6, Numbers 20:2). But for the nearly forty years between these two incidents, they were never without water. Why? Because

Miriam was such an outstanding person. In her merit, explains the midrash, God had mercy on the people, so wherever they were, a well appeared for them: "Miriam's well."

Why did Miriam deserve this honor? Miriam is most famous for leading the Jewish women in songs of praise after the crossing of the Red Sea. However, the specific merit associated with creating her well had to do with one of the deeds of her youth. She had been born, the second child in her family, at a time when Egyptian slavery had become very harsh. Pharaoh had decreed the slaughter of every male infant. The midrash says that after her birth, her father Amram divorced her mother, Yocheved, because he didn't want to bring any more children into this terrible life—particularly a boy, since the child would meet certain death. When Miriam learned of this, she told her father, "You are worse than Pharaoh! He decreed death only to male children; you have decreed against girls as well!" Amram saw her point and remarried Yocheved. Shortly after, she gave birth to Moses (*Sotah* 12a).

Miriam represents the ability to bring goodness even to the lowest levels of existence. Born when slavery was very harsh, when Jewish existence was near its lowest point, she was nevertheless able to see hope in the midst of difficulties. Like water flowing into every nook and crevice, her virtue and her faith in ultimate goodness flowed everywhere. Because of this merit, the Jews received the gift of "Miriam's well," which followed them throughout their travels in the desert.

Our own inner connection to Miriam's well is manifested physically in the "water," or flowing energy, of our body, which moves everywhere, into the lowest as well as the highest, the smallest as well as the largest vessels. Of the various forms of this energy, the Torah especially emphasizes two—the breath or *ruach*, and the blood or *dam*, as in "the blood is the life." Both flow throughout the body, just as waters and mist move in and around a mountain. Our task is to transform them, as did Miriam, into channels for goodness that will permeate even the lowest and densest levels of our being.

Following is a meditative visualization that can help bring into our consciousness the image of our bodies as flowing energy. This, like some other meditations in this chapter, is different from the meditations with body movements designed to accompany the morning blessings. You can reserve time for these as part of your morning routine, or before bed, or any time during the day that you want to work on your body-soul

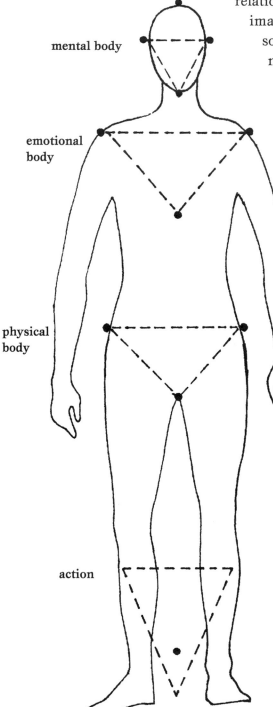

mental body

emotional body

physical body

action

relationship. The purpose is to induce positive imagery that will help us be in our bodies soulfully, nourishing ourselves from imaginative resources, rather than directly acting on the physical body through exercise.

You should not try to "master" the meditation by imagining the entire piece perfectly. Some people can easily visualize scenes and objects, while others are better at imagining sounds, smells, or touch. As you practice these meditations, use the inner "senses" that work best for you. With practice, meditating will become a fuller experience for you, one you can carry with you throughout your day.

Read through the entire meditation once to get the overall picture, then read it one step at a time (or have someone read it to you), experiencing each part slowly. You may prefer to have the meditations on tape, and you can use the form at the back of this book to order a tape that includes all the meditations in this book.

It may be helpful here to keep in mind the general diagram of the *sefirot* or energy points on the body, on this page. If you are unfamiliar with these, you may want to touch each of the points on your own body before you begin to bring them into your physical awareness. Light pressure or a slight massage can also aid the flow of energy through these nodal points.

Flowing Energy Meditation

Close your eyes. Imagine that you are walking across a meadow on a narrow path toward a forest on the other side of the meadow.

You can hear your breath as you walk, a calm steady rhythm that reminds you of the breath of life within. You can also sense your heartbeat, keeping the rhythm of your body steady, reminding you of your connection to God's infinite heartbeat.

The landscape unfolds in front of you, a lush forest in mountainous surroundings. Your hearing is keen. You can hear the sounds of birds singing in an angelic chorus, and a waterfall sounding its celebration of movement and power.

As you enter the forest, your eyes drink in the rich colors around you, the warm browns of the earth and tree trunks, the sun glistening on the leaves of the trees. You see the waterfall now. You can smell the green growing things, and the air tastes clean and fresh in your mouth.

You wander toward the waterfall, and you see a small, intimate spot where a tributary of the waterfall has created a separate sanctuary of its own. Here, warm water comes down quietly in a thinner stream and empties into a radiant pool. With the sun shining on it, it looks like a pool of divine light.

You walk nearer, and find there are stones under the waterfall where you can stand and catch its gentle spray. The water feels warm and soothing. As you sit down, the stones form a comfortable seat that cradles your body, and you rest in the warmth of the sun.

Breathe deeply and slowly. Bask in the pleasure of this moment and let yourself be taken care of in a profoundly loving way.

A gentle, warm rivulet from the waterfall flows down into the top of your head. Its color is sparkling gold.

Notice that divine cups are forming in your body at the points of the sefirot *to receive the liquid from the waterfall. One is at the top of your head, one at your right temple, one at your left, one at your throat. One forms at your right shoulder... your left shoulder... at your heart. A cup forms at your right hip, left hip, and one below the pubic bone. One rests between your feet.*

Now the golden liquid will flow down from above in a zigzag pattern to fill the cups. First it fills the cup at the top of your head, and the cup begins to overflow. Tilt your head to the right to let the liquid flow toward the cup at your right temple and fill it, until it overflows. Tilt your head slowly to the left, where the next cup waits to receive the life-giving flow. As this cup fills and spills over, straighten up and feel the fluid flowing into your throat.

For a moment, the flow stops. Imagine that the cups at your temples and your throat are the points of a triangle, which begins to glow with a warmth you can feel in your face. See it radiate with golden light, which relaxes any tension in your facial muscles. As you relax, the light also dissolves troublesome thoughts, old memories, and distractions. All the voices that usually clamor in your head fade away. The light allows wisdom and knowledge to manifest. This is the awakening of the mental or intellectual body.

The flow of warm liquid resumes. Tilt your upper body slightly to the right, so that the fluid can flow to the right shoulder. Slowly tilt toward the left, and imagine the shining liquid flowing to the left shoulder. As you straighten, feel it flow into your heart, and let your entire upper body feel the warmth.

Pause again for a moment. The cups at your shoulders and heart form a triangle that begins to radiate with silver light. The light dissolves any emotions that do not serve you today. Anger and fear melt away. Feel the light strengthen your emotional body by harnessing the wild nature of your emotions. The chest area fills with emotional balance, and you experience harmony within your emotional body.

The warm flow of liquid continues downward. Sway again to the right, this time allowing your side muscles to stretch, as the fluid goes to the cup at the right hip, then straighten up, pause a moment, and sway to the left, allowing the left hip to receive the warm liquid flow. Straighten again and allow the abdomen to be filled, flowing down to the cup below the pubic bone. The cups again form a triangle, which fills with copper light. As this light radiates in the pelvis, it dissolves any impurities or physical distractions. The copper light gives the body enduring power, and strengthens your connection to all the parts of your physical body that must be in place for God's energy to manifest.

Finally, see the last divine cup residing at your feet. This cup fills with all three colors—gold, silver, and copper. The light radiates out of the cup, up into the knees. This creates the last triangle, which represents our "walk," the way that mind, emotions, and body move together through the day. You actions are deeply affected when they are connected with divine

inspiration and soul energy. Feel the legs and feet grow warm and powerful.
See the waterfall of light running like a lightning bolt through the whole
body, and watch it form a pool at your feet. Sit at the pool as long as you
like. When you are ready to leave, stand up slowly, reminding yourself
that you are a stream of flowing energy. Stretch your arms up and out;
breathe deeply in and out. You may leave now, knowing that you can
return to this spot whenever you wish.

The Upper Torso and Upper Waters

Our body is water, a basic component of life as we know it. In the story
of creation, the Torah refers to two "waters," divided by God into upper
and lower waters on the second day of creation (Genesis 1:7). Our bodies reflect that division.[3]

The upper body is the center for breathing, which oxygenates our
bodies and is essential to all other bodily processes. The brain, for example, normally can function without oxygen for only four minutes. After
that time, a systemic crisis can seriously damage many of its functions.
We know how our bodies react to insufficient oxygen from the way we
feel when we exert ourselves until we are panting, or even when we
have a bad head cold that prevents proper breathing. Moreover, oxygen
is the food of the muscle: if a muscle cramps, it's literally choking. Air
has to be flowing to every movement of every muscle.

Besides the blood flowing through the brain, oxygen and air also go
through or near the sinus cavities, thereby directly contacting the brain
surface. The energies of the breath thus directly affect the central organ
of the nervous system, the brain.

Since increased oxygenation aids all the body's vital processes, exercise is very helpful, because it brings in more oxygen and improves lung
capacity. Moreover, it helps us expel more air, which in turn removes
impurities that tend to settle in the lungs if we do not breathe deeply
enough. The difference is similar to a stagnant pool compared to a flowing stream. One attracts disease and degeneration; the other produces
health in body, mind, and soul.

Besides its physical significance, however, the breath is universally
recognized in various spiritual traditions as essential to attuning the

body with the soul. In Judaism, this aspect of our physical nature is central to the very conception of the human being. The divine breath was the distinguishing feature of human creation: "And God breathed into his nostrils the breath of life" (Genesis 2:7). The fact that *ruach* means not only "breath," but also "spirit" and "wind," connects this physical process to the cosmic level of creation—the wind that carries moisture around the globe—and to the spiritual level, the *ruach* or divine energy that hovered over the waters at the beginning of creation (Genesis 1:2).

Breathing also moderates the spiritual "heat" of our body, so that the passions of the body do not overwhelm us. Rabbi Nachman of Breslov explains that the breath, *ruach,* is in the category of *"erech apaim,"* an expression that occurs in Psalm 145: "Gracious and merciful is my Lord, slow to anger (*erech apaim*) and great in kindness." *Erech apaim* is patience, and it is the long slow breath. A person who is angry, on the other hand, takes short breaths, just as we speak of someone "snorting" in anger. Long breaths extend one's patience and reflect, on the physical level, God's loving patience with us. For, as Rabbi Nachman says, God "extends his breath—sighing over man's weakness."[4]

The reference to patience and anger reminds us that, when we experience strong emotions, whether sorrow, excitement, or happiness, our breathing often changes. This suggests the connection between breath and heart, for in the heart—not only the physical organ, but also the surrounding area, with interaction between chest and lungs—most often reflects emotional changes. Of course, emotions are felt in other areas of the body, but the heart is the strongest center. As our tradition testifies in many places, the heart-lung region is the focus for and point of access to healing.

The book of Proverbs (15.13) says that "A happy heart makes a good countenance." The heart is directly connected to self-expression and relationships with others: when one's heart is physically healthy, one comes more easily to joy. And joy or spiritual illumination is reflected in one's face. The Bible also associates the word *lev* (heart) with rejoicing, comforting, depression, arrogance, hating, and desiring, as well as with understanding. When we ask God to "Open my heart in your Torah," we are asking for spiritual open-heart surgery. An "open heart" means that a person has become open to influences from others and, at the same time, enables them to see themselves more clearly.

This is also why exercise is so important for the whole person. Exercise helps the heart and lungs. But it also affects us emotionally. In fact, it is one of the major prescriptions for depression because when we don't exercise, we cannot easily release the tension caused by emotional stress. Unreleased tension can lead to a variety of unhealthy conditions, including being more susceptible to injury, accumulating fat in certain areas of the body, or chronic disease. Exercise can help the healthy body and soul to be more emotionally healthy as well.

Moreover, the heart is central because where the heart's desires turn, the body follows. Sometimes this can be negative, as when the heart envisions and chases after things that are not good for us. Then, as we say in the third paragraph of the *Shema,* "your eyes and your heart go astray." On the other hand, we can find contentment and happiness by balancing our physical and emotional needs. The mystics expressed this in the expression "Incense makes the heart happy." Incense is a metaphor for the breath becoming physical, through the sense of smell (which is said to be the most spiritual of the senses). The fragrance of incense produces much pleasure, but it is also smoke, signifying fire. Fire that becomes too intense, like an inferno, symbolizes harsh judgment. Similarly, our heart's desires may bring pleasure, but they may also lead to destructive behavior. When we moderate our emotions through the long, deep breath, we tone down the "fire" of passion. With discipline, such as regular in-and-out breathing, we can have the "incense that makes the heart happy" rather than the fire that only burns.

The idea of moderation and balance finds its expression in the left-right symmetry of our bodies. In the system of *sefirot,* they appear as the right and left "pillars." The right side expresses openness and giving, the left represents restraint and holding back. The healthy heart, in the center, is nourished by the balance in our emotions and actions, knowing when to extend ourselves and when to hold back, when to give and when to use discipline. Love, taken to an extreme, can be overpowering and destructive; too much discipline can be stifling. The goal is harmony, to balance both in the heart.

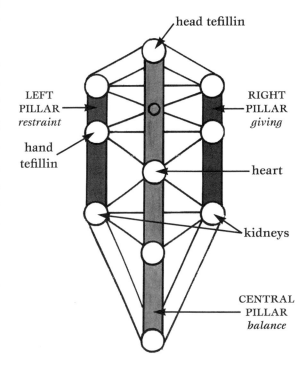

The heart is also a seat of understanding. The Torah speaks of the "wise-hearted" who were assigned to make beautiful things for the ancient place of worship (Exodus 31:6, 35:10). The Sages of the Talmud said, "The kidneys advise, the heart understands" (*Berachot* 61a). This goes against our culture's idea that the mind contains the intellect and the heart contains the emotions. From a Jewish perspective, the heart is connected to the mind: what the mind does affects the heart. *Tefillin* (phylacteries) symbolize this combination, for they are worn on the head where our cerebral capacities reside, *and* on the arm directly opposite the heart, the locus of a different form of understanding. Both are bound up with God.

Moreover, if one's mind is open to spiritual inspiration, the heart will yearn even more for God and Godly things. For, as the blessing following the morning *Shema* states, "Happy is the person who listens to Your commandments, and who places Your Torah and Your words *on his heart.*" Everything of significance must be "learned" in the heart. That is, it must be internalized.

According to Jewish mystical tradition, the heart is the central focus of the body, the "king" of all the organs. For example, using *gematria* (numerology based on Hebrew letters), the numerical value of *lev,* the Hebrew word for heart, is thirty-two. One of God's names, *Elohim,* appears thirty-two times in the story of creation in Genesis 1, a correspondence that suggests the centrality of the heart in creation. Moreover, the system of ten *sefirot* form a diagram with the heart at the center, representing a balanced energy system. Because the heart is spiritually the core of our very beings; it corresponds to the *Aron HaKodesh,* the Holy Ark, in the Holy of Holies in the Temple.[5]

The centrality of the heart in understanding and feeling, and the importance of the breath in physical and emotional life, make the heart-lung area a most important center of our internal energy. Rabbi Nachman uses a musical metaphor to describe the life-giving relationship of heart and lungs. The breath in the heart, he said, is like a wind playing a harp: "The *ruach* [breath, spirit] in the heart is the 'northern wind' *(ruach tzefonit)* which blew upon King David's harp of five strings." This breath can be compared to the *ruach* of God hovering over the surface of the water at the beginning of creation (Genesis 1:2). Moreover, in a play on words, he says that the *ruach **tzefon**it,* the harp-playing north wind, corresponds to the *ruach **hatzafun,*** the "hidden spirit," within the heart of man. Our breath, in other words, is like the creative spirit united with heartfelt desire, cherished in that moment before we enter upon creative activity in the world.

Awareness of breathing can expand our awareness of our heart-space and make it possible for us to open to our "hidden spirit." As we become aware of our breath, we start to become open to God's wisdom and creativity, and thus to our own.

Try the following meditation to develop more of this awareness.

Heart Meditation

Close your eyes. Imagine yourself sitting on a hill overlooking a beautiful meadow. The morning air is fresh, as after a rain. As you enjoy the clean smells around you, you are aware of how comfortable and serene you feel here. A gentle breeze soothes and caresses your body.

As you relax more deeply, you can hear a new sound, the hum of the ruach *or spiritual wind. It reminds you of the comforting sound of a loving mother's breath. As you listen, it begins to sound more musical, like a faraway harp. Again the sound rises and falls lightly, like the breath of a sleeping child, calm and sweet. Your own breath begins to match the rise and fall of the child's. Accept the sweetness. Let your breath become one with the child's. The sun bathes you in a golden light, and you feel very safe in this new place.*

Try to breathe in through your nose and out through your mouth. Try again—breathe in through your nose and out through your mouth. Listen...

The breeze around you now matches itself to your breath and enters your body, ever so gently. The coolness is like a refreshing mist, moving through your nose, your throat, your lungs, then through your upper body.

Focus on the throat area and begin to see there a small, five-stringed harp. Feel the strings activated by your breath and, as they vibrate, see their echo radiating energy, enlivening the throat center. Now sing out with a sound: A-a-a-h. Let the sound vibrate down into your heart. Place your hand on your chest, between your heart and your throat, and breathe out the sound again. Feel the vibration. Breathe in and this time, breathe out a prayer: "Baruch ata Adonai...." *Repeat three times.*

*Listen for the silence and feel the vibration in your body. Feel the heart awaken. Allow the breeze-*ruach*-prayer into your heart. Allow it to sweep* *clean any heaviness at your heart. Any sadness or hurt, disappointment, resentment, anger or pain crumbles into benign particles of dust. Remove all judgment of these emotions. They blow out of the heart freely, and you do not have to carry them anymore. Forgive yourself as God forgives you, with compassion and love. Feel the heart open.*

See the five-stringed harp appear now at your heart, and sing into your heart with your breath: "Baruch ata Adonai, rofeh chal basar umafli la-asot." *Repeat seven times. Listen for the silence once again. Feel the vibration cleanse and re-empower your heart, radiating out a healthy energy. The breeze carries the God-centered heart energy into all the other areas of your body, bringing a heightened awareness everywhere.*

Breathe deeply in and out three times. Feel a gentle vibration in the body as the energy flows out from your heart and breath into the limbs, organs and body parts, so that you may extend this divine energy and this prayer of healing out into the world today.

The Lower Torso and Lower Waters

The Torah and the sages attributed interesting features to certain organs of the lower half of the body. A comment in the Talmud, "The kidneys advise" (*Berachot* 61a), echoes King David's song: "I will bless the Lord who has advised me, even at night my kidneys instruct me" (Psalms 16.7). But this may seem very strange to us: What do the kidneys have to do with giving advice?

The Sages suggested that the right and left kidneys represent, respectively, the good and evil inclinations (*Berachot* 61a); another of their interpretations is that the two kidneys correspond to two aspects of our relationship to the divine: to fear God and to love God.[6] In both interpretations, these organs represent a system of duality or alternative courses of action. The role of these "advisers" is to signal to us how to choose between possible actions.

We can see this from a physical perspective: kidneys filter and detoxify, cleansing the blood, separating what is good for our bodies from what is bad. They monitor levels of sugar, salt, potassium, protein, and water. Further, atop the kidneys sit the powerful adrenal glands, which fuel our "fight or flight" reflex when a dangerous situation develops, and empower the body to go beyond its normal range of reactions. So, along two different dimensions, the kidney area represents decision-making.

The kidneys symbolize the whole process of separating the useful from the not-useful. This process is essential to our physical existence. On the spiritual level, it is the aspect of refinement and clarification.

Yet the purification systems of the lower body operate in a way that is completely involuntary and instinctual. We can to some extent voluntarily increase or decrease the speed of our breath and expand our lungs more or less. But there is normally nothing we can do consciously to affect the processes of digestion and excretion except by such unusual means as laxatives or emetics. Even the muscles of the abdominal area are less sensitive. In fitness workouts, we can work on strengthening the abdominal wall only by feeling it externally (with hand pressure) and by using other muscles, because kinesthetic awareness in this area is difficult to develop.

Moreover, we assume that things are going well with these organs when we don't get any feedback from them. If we have pain, discomfort, or changes in excretions, we know something is wrong; but they do not automatically feed us positive information. They are demanding, however: When they need attention, we must respond.

The involuntary, silent and unresponsive nature of these organs is part of the reason they have been categorized as our "lower" self. In addition, the lower half of our body contains the sexual organs, which also function instinctually in many respects, normally out of conscious control. Whether it is unexpected or unwanted sexual arousal, or the regular cycles of a woman's menstruation, these organs also go their way, at times disrupting our conscious lives in ways that our "higher" selves would sometimes prefer to suppress.

Our desire to control our bodies—even while much of it is not subject to conscious control—has encouraged negative attitudes especially toward our "lower" halves. No wonder, then, that fat and cellulite tend to settle there, that we more often have *lower* back problems, and that many psychological symptoms manifest as problems with intake or digestion of food, or with sexuality. The task of healing ourselves includes recovering a sensibility for our lower torso and bringing it into relationship with the conscious self.

Let's look again at the body. If we first consider the parts of the body that are easier to understand, we can gain a better sense for the lower region. In the head are right and left brain, with eyes, ears, and nostrils taking in information from the world. In the center is the mouth, the organ of taste and preliminary digestion, and also of speech, which connects with the outside world. This triangle of right, left, center corresponds to the *sefirot* of the head.

In the upper torso are the right and left lungs, with the heart in the center of this part of the body. These again correspond to three *sefirot*. The lungs are the major processor of air, the inspiriting breath *(ruach)* that nourishes the whole body, while the heart moves the blood, with its connection to the vital soul *(nefesh)*. As the seat of emotions, the heart region is a place of "communication" as well. This area also contains the female breasts, which extend toward the outer world, both producing milk to nourish the infant and attracting the male.

Now we can see the lower torso also as a triangle. The kidneys are the principal processing organs, not by receiving directly from outside but by purifying what is already within. In the center are the reproductive organs, which again "communicate" with the outside world, attracting and connecting with the opposite sex and, in the woman, bringing forth new life. The lower body also includes the thighs, the strongest muscles in our body. This "support system" of physical life symbolically represents wealth, which also concerns our relationship to the outside world.

The three triangles are wonderfully analogous. The receivers and processors are on the right and left sides of the body, and the connectors are in the center, with each representing a different level of functioning.

Rabbi Nachman taught that the area of the kidneys corresponds to the *keruvim* (cherubim) on the cover of the Ark in the *Mishkan*.[7] These *keruvim* were two winged figures who, it was said, embraced one another when the Jewish people were in harmony with one another and with God, but turned their faces away from one anoth-

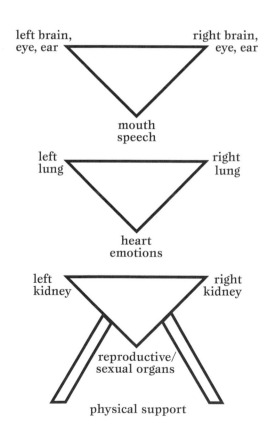

left brain, eye, ear — right brain, eye, ear

mouth
speech

left lung — right lung

heart
emotions

left kidney — right kidney

reproductive/
sexual organs

physical support

...Even the ordinary Israelite is a member of "the nation of *Cohanim*" and may eat of sacrifices...; therefore their holy bodies also serve to consume the sacrifices.

Thus, before offering his daily prayers to *Hashem*, he cleanses his hands: "I wash my hands in cleanliness, and I go around your *Mizbeach* [altar], *Hashem*, that I may make the voice of thanksgiving to be heard, and tell of your wondrous works" (Psalms 26: 6-7).

When the Israelite puts upon himself his garments, he can think of...the *Cohen* that dons the sacerdotal vestments;

when he washes his hands before prayer he is imitating the *Mitzvah* of *Cohanim* to wash their hands and feet before performing *Avodah* (Exodus 30:20-21);

and when he purifies his body before praying ("One that needs to relieve himself is forbidden to pray"—*Berachot* 23a), he may utilize the model of removing the ash from the *Mizbeach* before bringing offerings upon it...

The kosher food...is then consumed on the holy altar of the Israelite body.

—*Rabbi Avigdor Miller*, A Kingdom of Cohanim *(1994)*[8]

er when relationships were not good. Inside the Ark were the *luchot*, stone tablets containing the Ten Commandments, the essence of God's communication to human beings. In addition, the voice of God came to Moses from between the *keruvim*: "I will speak to you from above the ark-cover, from between the two *keruvim* that are on the ark of testimony" (Exodus 25:22). Each triangle on the body corresponds to the "triangle" of the Ark: the "processors" to the *keruvim* who sensed the energy of the Jewish people, the "connectors" to the words of God in the Ark.

This helps us see more clearly how to relate to the organs of the lower torso. Just as we care about what we see and hear, just as we want clean fresh air in our lungs, so the substances that we process in our lower body must be kept clear and healthy. In particular, we need to make disciplined decisions about physical intake. We know that addictive behavior or uncontrolled consumption of such substances as sugar, salt, caffeine or alcohol affects the kidneys. Excessive intake of such substances also often reflects inner, emotional disturbances, such as anger or fear which we may deny. Such emotional imbalances affect our internal "adviser" and processor, the kidneys. The ability to discipline one's intake of food and other substances mirrors the ability to feel, understand, and channel one's hidden emotions in a healthy way.

For this reason, *kashrut* (the practice of eating only kosher food from kosher vessels) helps every act of eating become a way we can align ourselves with God. In addition, God asks that we also select *healthy* kosher food to fulfill the *mitzvah* of taking care of our vital souls. The right amount of food is important as well: As the Rambam taught eight centuries ago, the main principle that should guide our eating is moderation. The stomach is normally only the size of the fist, so we don't need to eat as much as we think we do. If someone is overeating (or has a great fondness for unhealthy substances), that person is not being "filled up" in a spiritual way. We have to be patient, gentle, and loving with ourselves, and create a spiritually nourishing environment around food.

If you don't have a problem with food or nutrition, keep doing what you're doing. If you do, here are a few simple rules to provide a positive atmosphere.

- ☐ Try eating one plate of food with moderate portions, three times a day.

- ☐ Eat fruit or vegetables for snacks.

- ☐ Leave a little on your plate "for God," as an exercise in mindful eating. God will rejoice that you made a spiritual connection through something so ordinary.

- ☐ Set a nice table for yourself, sit down, and eat slowly.

- ☐ Try to eat healthy, low-fat foods, but don't deprive yourself of foods you truly enjoy.

- ☐ Take pleasure from your food, but have something interesting to do or study after your meal so you won't overindulge. If you do want to eat more, explore your need for excess food.

- ☐ Say a prayer—personal or traditional—before and after you eat. This encourages a spirit of gratitude, and aligns us with the *mitzvah* of "You shall eat and be satisfied, and bless Adonai your God" (Deuteronomy 8:10).

Sexuality, the "connecting" force in the lower body, also has its mirrors in the "higher" self. Sexual arousal may get out of control, and in our society it is easy to treat sexuality casually. But we know that our sexual life is far more healthy when we are connected emotionally to our partner and when we are engaged in it with full mental awareness. This means involving all the regions of our bodies with their distinctive contributions. Some people—more often women—tend to make connections between the sexual area and the heart center, choosing sexual relationships according to their emotional reactions to their partners. Others—more often men—tend to be guided more by their sensory impressions and the associated thoughts and images, connecting the sexual area with the head. Both are powerful, and neither is complete: All three regions must be connected in order for sexuality to be meaningful. When we think further of the potential to bring new life into the world through the work of the sexual organs, being fully connected to the sexual act assumes even more importance.

Moreover, as we become more fully aware of ourselves as complex emotional, spiritual, and sexual beings, we discover that the search for intimacy with another person is part of our search for our own deeper self. Indeed, psychologists have analyzed "romantic love" in almost spiritual terms: People who are attractive to us frequently embody aspects of our "lost" selves, namely the emotions and desires we felt our parents would not accept. As a result, these potential partners appear to be the "other half" of our own soul. We are usually quite oblivious to the fact that our lover is offering what we are missing or are afraid of in ourselves. Thus, when we "fall in love," we often fall prey to the illusion that the other person will complete our lives. And the reason that romantic love fades soon after marriage is that another person can never substitute for truly rediscovering our own soul. Marriage then has to be reconstituted on a more loving and giving, rather than merely self-reflective, foundation.[9]

The powerful energy we feel in sexual attraction is a reflection, in the ordinary world, of our spiritual need to complete ourselves. The emptiness we sometimes feel when relationships are not satisfying is, on a deeper level, a spiritual hunger, our need for a loving relationship with God. So, the mystics say, sexuality is connected not only to the lower body but also to the crown of the head and the higher levels of the soul. To have a healthy sexuality, we need to be fully connected to all aspects of ourselves, including our divine souls. Then we can work with a partner on deeper emotional and spiritual growth, on unselfishly loving one another, and sexuality can express our divine source.

The hips and thighs are the strong and stable support for the body. In Jewish mysticism, they symbolize material support or wealth. But the desire for wealth can also get out of control, especially amid the extraordinary resources and great affluence of American society. Rabbi Nachman taught that the desire for wealth is the most difficult desire to correct. It is a great challenge to achieve humility and awe of God in face of our cravings for power, wealth, and material possessions. In order to achieve humility in the face of wealth, we sometimes have to undergo painful experiences. Recall that Jacob, who had become rich while working as a shepherd for his uncle Laban, injured his left hip while wrestling with an angel (Genesis 31:1-13, 32:25). The midrash tells us that the angel represented Esau, his brother, who had devoted himself to acquiring wealth and power. Jacob had pursued a different path, but still had to "wrestle" with the desire. Thus, the Sages tell us, being attentive to how one gets and spends money is as important as the food one eats and the way one acts in intimate relationships, for these too reflect our relationship with God.

The lower torso represents energy that is passionate, driving, creative, powerful. But clear guidelines for a healthy, balanced use of this power are rare today. We are bombarded with contradictory messages. Magazine racks advertise rigid fad diets, while restaurants offer combinations of foods and desserts that would strain anyone's digestive capacity. Fitness programs try to beat the hips and thighs into shape while sedentary activity, such as riding in cars or sitting in front of computer screens or televisions, occupies ninety percent of our waking hours. Physicians tell us that plenty of sexual activity is healthy, while disease centers portray specters of future infertility and death due to an alarming rise in sexually transmitted diseases. The multiplicity of ways we are encouraged to spend money would be beyond the wildest fantasies of anyone from any previous century.

These cultural messages were called "temptations" in previous centuries. Metaphorically, they are forms of "slavery to Pharaoh in Egypt." We are being asked to devote our physical energy and power of action to a multiplicity of alien "rulers." Judaism's response to these challenges is that we should not try to ignore the body or eliminate its desires, but refine them in a spiritual direction, just as the kidneys and digestive organs refine and distribute our intake of food and drink, fueling our bodies in the precise amounts needed. We need to find ways to channel our physical energy and passion toward the Divine.

On the physical level, we try to take in healthy and kosher foods and condition our bodies through exercise to use as much of the nourishment as possible. Remember that the lower torso needs action and movement, just as the upper torso needs the benefits of breathing and circulation. You can creatively develop an exercise program of your own, or use one that already exists. Walk, swim, dance, do yoga, or run—the list is endless, and you can find what you like best. The main thing is to do it regularly and daily, whether you start with five minutes a day or fifteen, and try to increase it to thirty minutes. Do it out of love for your body—and because you want to be closer with God. Be patient and gentle with your own resistance, remembering that God wants you to care for the body, this special Divine gift. Gradually, as you begin to pay attention to your body, it will tell you what it needs.

Emotionally, we can learn to clear ourselves of past resentments, grudges, and jealousies, refining our relationships with others. On the mental level, we can try to think and plan before we act, and work on creating a realistic discipline for our lives. For our whole selves, we can develop positive images through relaxed meditations.

Particularly with the lower torso, we have few positive images. Try the meditative visualization below to develop a fuller sense of your lower body.

Healing Stream Meditation

Take a moment to quiet your body and bring it to a place of stillness. Turn your thoughts inward and see yourself walking down a rustic path into a serene woody setting. As you walk, you come upon a sparkling stream of running waters. You can see that this is a special stream, for it is laced with strands of golden light from the sun's rays.

A quiet steam is rising slowly from the waters; the stream is fed by a hot spring. As you close your eyes and bring in the fresh smells of the forest, you hear the soothing sound of the stream, singing of peace.

The stream seems to be inviting you into its waters. You slip off your shoes and step onto the warm earth. As you enter the water, you feel firm, smooth sand on the bottom of the stream. You sit down in the water, and the earth underneath makes a soft seat for you.

The waters move swiftly around and through your body. They begin to cleanse your lower back of pain and tension. Any tightness, stress, or discomfort in the abdomen is washed away. The area of the groin is washed, and the healing waters move around and through your thighs, knees, calves, ankles, feet and toes. The entire lower half of your body feels free and clear. Wiggle your toes and gently rock your hips from side to side. Breathe in deeply, then exhale completely.

Now you notice again the strands of golden light that sparkle on these waters. They feel warm and highly energized. The strands of gold begin to move into your body, filling the places that have been cleansed. The golden strands begin to fill the energy centers, the sefirot of the lower body. First the golden light forms a ball of light at the right hip. You feel the energy of raw physical power, like the rushing water itself, or like a runner gathering energy to push off from the starting block with the right leg.

Next the golden strands form a ball at the left hip. This ball reflects back and stabilizes the energy from the right, as the rushing waters are formed into a shape by the banks of the river, or as the runner balances on the left leg.

Then the golden strands form a ball of light just below the pubic bone. This is the manifestation of creative energy, like the river flowing in its channel that can power a generator or push a barge down the stream, or like the athlete with grace and speed running a race. This triangle is the pivotal point of the physical body, stabilizing and balancing our powerful instincts in the right direction. Now, purified and connected to God's will, it can empower you for all the actions you take.

You have received all that you need for now, and you can return to the stream whenever you need to. Slowly step out of the stream and give thanks for this new awareness. Your clothes dry immediately and you put your shoes back on. Feel the new strength of the lower torso as you walk. Breathe deeply in, and breathe out completely. Feel the gratitude in your newly empowered body.

Most of all, we need to connect our body, mind, and spirit so they can help one another. Disciplined energy, whether mental, emotional, or physical, returns goodness to the heart, the center of our being. When we put our desires in the context of Godly service, positive energy fills the heart, the center of our being, and the upper and lower waters are united.

In making our bodies, God created, in a sense, the perfect *challah* (braided bread). God thought up the image (*tzelem elohim,* the "image of God"), and gathered dust of the earth. To this, God added "water," the flowing energy from "Miriam's well," all the vital energy that keeps us alive, the province of the *nefesh.* God breathed into it the *ruach,* the breath that makes it expand, and then allowed us to "bake" it, with the heat of our actions and passions. Now it is up to us to keep the energy moving, to make it vital and soulful in every area of our lives.

The Miraculous Body:
Asher Yatzar with Movement and Meditation

Recognizing the spiritual significance behind each region and organ of our body gives a different dimension to our physical experience each day. As we each develop in our own personal consciousness of the body through attention and meditations such as the ones suggested above, the prayer *Asher Yatzar* also acquires deeper meaning. We can begin to fulfill the promise of the Messianic age, "In my flesh I will see God" (Job 19:27).

Now we can return to the morning blessings and do the prayer with greater consciousness. The movements are small, with emphasis on concentrated awareness of the inside of the body rather than large external movement. Again, we suggest you say the prayer aloud, do the following exercise, saying it quietly to yourself, and then the brief meditation.

בָּרוּךְ אַתָּה, יהוה, אֱלֹהֵינוּ מֶלֶךְ הָעוֹלָם, אֲשֶׁר יָצַר
אֶת-הָאָדָם בְּחָכְמָה, וּבָרָא בוֹ נְקָבִים נְקָבִים, חֲלוּלִים
חֲלוּלִים. גָּלוּי וְיָדוּעַ לִפְנֵי כִסֵּא כְבוֹדֶךָ, שֶׁאִם יִפָּתֵחַ אֶחָד
מֵהֶם, אוֹ יִסָּתֵם אֶחָד מֵהֶם, אִי אֶפְשָׁר לְהִתְקַיֵּם וְלַעֲמוֹד
לְפָנֶיךָ. בָּרוּךְ אַתָּה, יהוה, רוֹפֵא כָל-בָּשָׂר וּמַפְלִיא לַעֲשׂוֹת.

*Ba-ruch a-ta, A-do-nai, El-o-he-nu, Me-lech ha-o-lam, a-sher ya-tzar
et ha-a-dam b'hokh-mah, u-va-ra vo ni-ka-vim ni-ka-vim, cha-lu-
lim cha-lu-lim, ga-lu-i v'ya-du-a lif-ne chi-say ch'vo-de-cha, she-im
yi-pa-te-ach e-chad me-hem, o yi-sa-tem e-chad me-hem, iy ef-shar
l'hit-ka-yem v'la-a-mod l'fa-ne-cha. Ba-ruch a-ta, A-do-nai, ro-feh
chal ba-sar u-maf-li la-a-sot.*

Blessed are You, Adonai our God, Ruler of the Universe, who has
formed the human being with wisdom, and has created in us a multitude
of openings and cavities. It is obvious and known before Your glorious
Throne that if but one of these were open [that should be closed], or
one were closed [that should be open], we would be unable to stay alive
and stand before You. Blessed are You, Adonai who heals all flesh and
does wonders!

"...A multitude of openings and cavities."

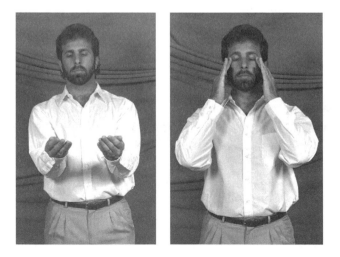

1. Sit with crossed legs or on a firm chair, or you may stand. We first acknowledge the five senses, the miraculous "openings" God has given us to perceive the world. Touch your fingertips to your thumbs to acknowledge the sense of touch. Then place your fingertips on your eyes. Slowly and with consciousness place them on your nostrils, feeling your breath. Place them on your ears

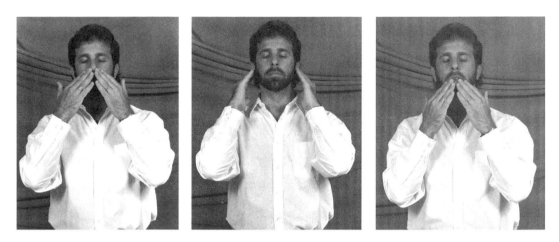

and acknowledge your miraculous ability to turn vibrations of the air into meaningful sounds. Finally, place your fingertips on your lips and appreciate the pleasures you have from your sense of taste. This is the time also to take note of the miraculous openings that rid our body of waste to keep us healthy; and of those that bring forth the miracle of life.

"...Before Your glorious Throne."

2. Breathe deeply. Reach both hands over your head and bring them down as if pulling the light of God down into your physical body. Stretch your palms wide open and place them near your face. Be aware of how sensitive they become to your own body heat.

Now, without touching your body (hands an inch or two away from body surface, palms facing toward your body), move your hands down

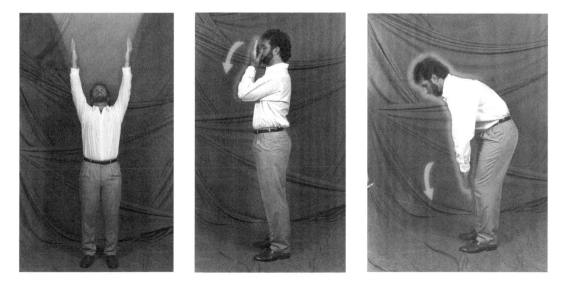

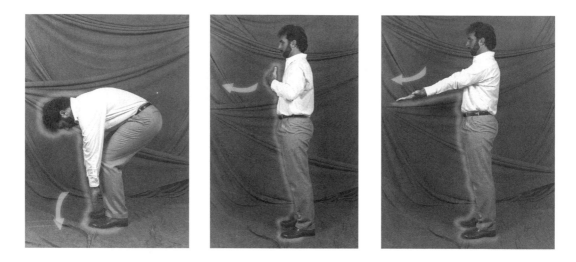

the front of your body, all the way to your legs and feet. When you reach the feet, slowly move your hands back up to the area of your heart. Open your hands in front of you, in the humble position of receiving.

"Who heals all flesh and does wonders."

3. Extend your arms forward. Turn your left palm up and place your right palm over it, palm down, without touching. With your right palm about an inch from the surface of your skin, move your right hand along the inner surface of your left arm all the way to your heart. Repeat on the other side, moving your left hand along the inner surface of your right arm to your heart. Open both palms in front of you, again receiving God's light. Continue holding the palms open as you do the meditation that follows.

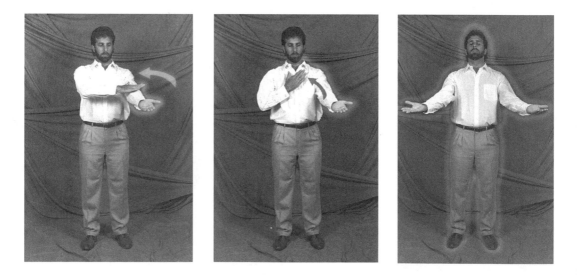

Meditation

Continue to breathe deeply. Humbly thank God for this miraculous physical form, a Divine creation to house our souls. Metaphorically, God has made the perfect challah. *The body is an awesome design, crafted with openings that cleanse us and cavities that house the organs that keep us alive. Although we never feel the great work of these powerful internal organs, we know they are vibrating powerfully to create the harmonic symphony of life. We humbly appreciate God's unceasing desire to care for the well-being of these human bodies, and God's ability to heal our pain if we reach out to our Divine Source.*

בָּרוּךְ אַתָּה, יְיָ אֱלֹהֵינוּ, מֶלֶךְ הָעוֹלָם, אֲשֶׁר קִדְּשָׁנוּ בְּמִצְוֹתָיו
וְצִוָּנוּ לַעֲסוֹק בְּדִבְרֵי תוֹרָה. וְהַעֲרֶב-נָא, יהוה אֱלֹהֵינוּ, אֶת-דִּבְרֵי
תוֹרָתְךָ בְּפִינוּ, וּבְפִי עַמְּךָ בֵּית יִשְׂרָאֵל, וְנִהְיֶה אֲנַחְנוּ וְצֶאֱצָאֵינוּ,
וְצֶאֱצָאֵי עַמְּךָ בֵּית יִשְׂרָאֵל, כֻּלָּנוּ יוֹדְעֵי שְׁמֶךָ וְלוֹמְדֵי תוֹרָתֶךָ
לִשְׁמָהּ. בָּרוּךְ אַתָּה, יהוה, הַמְלַמֵּד תּוֹרָה לְעַמּוֹ יִשְׂרָאֵל.

בָּרוּךְ אַתָּה, יהוה, אֱלֹהֵינוּ מֶלֶךְ הָעוֹלָם, אֲשֶׁר בָּחַר בָּנוּ מִכָּל
הָעַמִּים, וְנָתַן לָנוּ אֶת תּוֹרָתוֹ. בָּרוּךְ אַתָּה, יהוה, נוֹתֵן הַתּוֹרָה.

Blessed are You, Adonai, our God, Ruler of the universe, who has sanctified us with Your commandments and commanded us to be absorbed in words of Torah.

Please, Adonai our God, make the words of Your Torah sweet in our mouths, and in the mouth of Your people the House of Israel. May it be that we and our offspring and the offspring of Your people the House of Israel, all of us, know Your Name and study Your Torah for its own sake. Blessed are You, Adonai, the Teacher of Torah to Your people Israel.

Blessed are You, Adonai our God, Ruler of the universe, who chooses us from all peoples and gives us Your Torah. Blessed are You, who gives the Torah.

To practice the prayer with its movement and meditation, please turn to page 90.

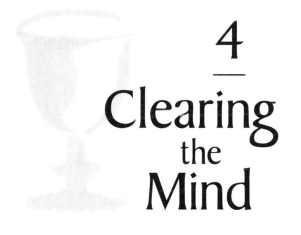

4

Clearing
the
Mind

EACH MORNING, after thanking God for our wondrous bodies, we say blessings over the Torah, another Divine gift to us.

We thank God not only for the gift of the Torah itself but also, and first, for the commandment to *study* Torah. Only by active learning, not mere reading or recitation, can we attune our minds to our souls. Thus these three blessings are about God's teaching (the literal meaning of "Torah") and our learning in order to shape our minds in a soulful direction.

Judaism has always held education in high esteem. But the phrase "Torah for its own sake" in the second blessing above suggests an additional feature: One should engage in Torah study without anticipating its final results, since such study is intrinsically a healthy activity for the mind.

To understand how this is so, we have to understand how our minds work. So let us ask ourselves: Is the mind an ally in our spiritual search? Or is it an obstacle? To find out, let's return to how we start the morning.

The Cluttered Mind

The alarm rings. For many of us, our first thought is, "Oh, no! It can't be morning already." The mind becomes negative almost as soon as it is conscious!

It's not easy to get up. But let's say you do manage to say *Modeh Ani* before your feet hit the floor. You then wash your hands, and do the morning stretches. Your body is functioning a little better, but your mind may not be. It's quite common to hear a chorus of voices:

"Remember all the things you were going to do yesterday? You didn't get half of them done, did you? Do you think you can do any better today? Ha!"

"Your wife [or your husband, or your boss] is still mad at you. You're going to have to deal with that today."

"Why don't you get organized at night so you don't have to do so much in the morning?"

"How many years do you think you have left? Since you're going to die someday anyway, why not go back to bed?"

This happens because thoughts have no inherent direction. To prove this to yourself, sit and watch your thoughts with no task before you. You will find yourself creating strings of associations, streams of thoughts, images and phrases that meander this way and that, until you wonder where you started. This means that once a given thought is formed, it can be manipulated in innumerable ways, from expressing it in mathematical formulas to using it in political propaganda. But what direction your mind will take, if left to its own devices, cannot be determined.

If we want to use thought as a vehicle for healing and wholeness, the mind must become clear of distractions and able to focus on what is healthy, balanced, and empowering. When we sweep our minds clean, we actually become more intelligent. People who overcome addictions or chronic depression not only report that they feel smarter, but perform better on intelligence tests. We are all able to use more of our brain power, if we only practice.

The Baal Shem Tov, the eighteenth-century founder of Hasidism, expressed this idea when he taught us to clear away the debris of our lives:

> The earth is full of treasures, but the treasures are often buried deep. It is necessary to dig for them, and when you discover them, you still have to clear away the impurities, refine them or polish them, as in the case of gold or a diamond and the like. So is every Jew full of wonderful treasures of character—modesty, kindness, and other natural traits—but sometimes they are buried deep and covered by soil and dust which have to be cleared away.

In our minds, too, a great deal of debris keeps us busy all day. One of the purposes of meditation and prayer is to train our mind to focus on what we decide is important. As we hone this ability, we learn to ignore the trivial and turn to God.

Further, our emotional attachments often return us again and again to disturbing, "obsessional" thoughts. If you had a misunderstanding with your spouse, or if you have a court case coming up, you may see your thoughts circling around, continually returning to rehearse or re-imagine conversations and encounters that are emotionally significant to you. Emotionally charged situations that are not dealt with during the day will occupy our minds at night, causing sleeplessness or disturbing dreams.

Emotions block the mind's clear, healthy activity in several ways. We can see some of these if we imagine our mental processes and our ability to learn as points along a Ladder of the Mind. The steps on this ladder are like the Four Sons of the Passover Hagaddah. From the Son Who Doesn't Know How to Ask, to the Wise Son who asks about all the details of the ceremony and laws, we embody each of them in our approaches to learning. As mental attitudes, these "Sons" are facts of life. Without being judgmental, we can recognize that they are different levels we each experience at different times, in facing life's various challenges. In this way, we can begin to accept our own minds and our own unique approaches to thinking about reality.

The Wise Son, who has a thirst and passion for knowledge, seeks more and more profound learning. His is the awakened mind. We are like this when we have already done some solid work in a particular subject, and we feel confident about it. This is the mind at its best, though it has the potential to lead to intellectual arrogance. We would like to have the mental capabilities of the Wise Son all the time, but each of us is limited by our talents and experience to a few areas in which we can confidently plow ahead. To be truly Wise is also to accept one's limitations.

The Wicked Son has intelligence, but he is unable to change. He asks about the Passover Seder, "What is this to *you?*" But he excludes himself from the query. He recognizes that he is being confronted with something that might require him to change part of his life if he accepted it as truth. Rather than confront the pain of change, he rejects it: This is something for *you,* he concludes, but not for me. He ends up denying that he is part of a broader community.

We are like this when we judge the validity of other people's experiences. Rather than admit that we have something to learn, we would rather draw a line between "us" and "them." In matters of spirituality, this often comes out as, "If you believe that, you're a fool," or "They live in an unreal world." We need a larger concept of ourselves in the world, recognizing that, as the second-century sage Ben Zoma said, "Who is wise? He who learns from everyone" (*Avot* 4: 1).

The Simple Son just says, "What's this?" He is open and interested; he has a receptive innocence and a willingness to learn. But he is a complete beginner. He needs to acquire very basic knowledge in a subject. When we approach a new subject as adults, the thought of being beginners is quite daunting. We feel we don't have time to "start over." It helps to recognize that life is always a process of growth and development. We will always be learning. So, "if not now, when?" The key to such a humbling experience is patience. We must be kind to ourselves and recognize that small steps, performed regularly and with perseverance, will lead us to the goal.

The Son Who Doesn't Know How to Ask is asleep. He might as well have dropped in from Mars. Unfocused and in a kind of mental limbo, he needs someone else to take his hand and "open the subject for him." We are like this when we become numb to ourselves. Whether through negative experiences in childhood, self-abuse, or sheer avoidance, part of our mind has become paralyzed. What we need, most of all, is a relationship of caring. We need to trust that others can sometimes see us more clearly than we see ourselves, and that we can turn to them for advice.

The challenge is to recognize which step of the Ladder of the Mind we are on, then accept it and do what is necessary to heal the mind. When we are open-minded, when we are willing to be "beginners," and when we trust those who are offering their help, then we will be able to wholeheartedly pursue deeper knowledge.

Your Words Sweet in Our Mouths

The ultimate aim of our knowing activity is God. As Jewish philosophy has taught since the Rambam's great work eight centuries ago, God in essence is without attributes, so we can't know or meditate on God directly. Knowing God means knowing the Divine within all its created manifestations. That knowledge develops as we develop spiritually, through the work of learning "Torah."

A-sher kid'sha-nu b'mitz-vo-tav, v'tzi-va-nu la-a-sok b'di-vrei To-rah, "Who has sanctified us with Your commandments, and commanded us to be absorbed in words of Torah." The first of the morning blessings over the Torah tells us, in effect, that our main business, our "occupation," is Torah. Not our career, nor our company, but the study and practice of Torah. The Sages taught that the habitual reading and studying of sacred literature is a purifying influence. If the role of Jews is to be a kingdom of *cohanim* and a light to the nations, we can continually renew ourselves in that role by studying Torah.

We say this blessing with the other morning blessings rather than waiting until we actually sit down to study, before we might even accidentally speak words of Torah. This reminds us how precious is the knowledge. The Talmud warns that if one studies, but does not say the blessing, one's children will not be scholars! Why? The spirit of gratitude would be missing, and children, with their intuitive apprehension of their parents' true values and priorities, would recognize this and not be interested in Torah themselves. Tradition says that the neglect of this blessing was also one of the reasons for the destruction of the Temple in Jerusalem in 70 C.E., Too many scholars were not learning out of love of God and desire for the Divine Light, but out of egotism or habit. Thus the blessing should be said first thing in the morning, intending that it will apply to everything one learns during the day.

These first two blessings particularly refer to the *Torah sheb'al peh*, the Oral Torah. This includes the entirety of Mishnah and Talmud down to the responsa of the great sages of the present century. In this way, Torah can continue its powerful influence, because the Oral Torah makes the teachings relevant to everything in life. As the commentators to a contemporary *siddur* point out, "Without it [the Torah], man cannot know God's will; with it, he can penetrate the wisdom of the Creator Himself." This also hints as to why the blessings over studying Torah come first: The Torah will mean nothing to us unless we discover how to put it into effect in our lives.[1]

V'ha-a-rev-na, ...et di-vrei to-rat'cha b'fi-nu, u-v'fi am'cha beit Yis-ra-el. The second part of the blessing is actually a prayer: "Please make the words of Your Teaching sweet in our mouth, and in the mouth of Your people, the House of Israel." This beautiful phrase reminds us that mind is not merely an abstract process, but a physical one as well, since it involves the organ of the mouth. The power of thought is intimately connected with the power of speech. In fact, from the time a child learns to speak, if not earlier, waking thoughts are connected to words and word-images. Even in sleep, our dreams sometimes involve plays on words, demonstrating that even at unconscious levels, we are beings who speak. To influence our minds spiritually, we must work with our speech. This is one reason why Torah is traditionally studied with the text being read or recited aloud.

V'ni-yeh a-nach-nu v'tze-tza-e-nu v'tze-tza-ei am'cha beit Yis-ra-el, ku-la-nu yo-dei sh'me-cha v'lom-dei to-ra-te-cha lish-mah, "May it be that we and our offspring and the offspring of Your people the House of Israel, all of us, know Your Name and study Your Torah for its own sake." This passage refers to the next step in our relationship with God. As we commit ourselves to being occupied with Torah and receiving the light of revelation, the words become so pleasurable to us that we can't help sharing them with others, and especially with our children and grandchildren. It reminds us also to look for the sweetness in the words we study, and to get involved with them as a way to be part of the community and the whole Jewish people, whose mission is to spread the knowledge of God.

Ultimately, we are asking for the words to help seal a relationship in which Torah becomes an intimate conversation between each of us and God. Rabbi Yochanan, a Sage in the Talmud, used a quote from the

Song of Songs to describe this blessing: "Friendship is sweeter than wine." The blessing we say over the Oral Torah reflects the idea that our continuing conversation with God is sweeter even than the wine that is purely from God, the written Torah.

A-sher ba-char ba-nu mi-kal ha-a-mim, v'na-tan la-nu et To-ra-to, "Who has chosen us from all peoples and gives us the Torah." The blessings over the Torah conclude with the same blessing that is said by a person called up for an *aliyah* (a portion of the day's Torah reading) when the Written Torah is read in public. This reminds us that we have been carriers of the Torah through the centuries, and that God continues to give us this purpose in life. In addition, by using the present tense (*natan,* "gives"), this blessing reminds us that the Torah is still being given every day. Every day, we can imagine ourselves standing at Sinai, hearing the Ten Commandments, and recommitting ourselves to learn and practice them.

Following a blessing over an action, one should perform that action immediately. Here the *siddur* inserts three selections from the Torah—one from Chumash (Numbers 6:24-26, known as the Priestly Blessing), one from Mishnah *Peah,* and one from Talmud *Shabbat.* Thus we actually learn a small piece of the holy words for which we have just thanked God.

By saying these blessings with *kavannah* (spiritual intent), we turn our mind to the true Source of knowledge, and its earthly manifestation in the Written and Oral Torah. We can daily prepare ourselves to be receivers of God's light. We take the opportunity to empty our minds of chatter, worries, and obsessions, and fill ourselves instead with reading and discussing Torah. We pray that our minds can be used for spiritual growth.

By becoming willing to learn, even just to say the words, we also create the beginning of a trusting relationship with God. We trust that the knowledge we receive will be the light needed for our path that day. In this respect, the Torah is like the manna that fell in the desert to feed the Jewish people after they came out of Egypt. Manna appeared every morning, like dew, on top of the ground. It had a sweet flavor, and could be gathered and made into wafers or cakes. God told the people that they had to collect every day the exact amount of manna needed for the number of people in their households,. On Friday, they were to collect a double portion, one for that day and one for Shabbat. Under no circumstances could they hoard it, because it would become full of worms. In this way, God taught the people to trust that their sustenance would be provided day by day, so they should live in the present and not worry about the future.

Manna was given to the people because of the greatness of Moses. The midrash says it tasted like any food one wanted at the time, and so it satisfied their physical desires. In the same way, the Torah came through Moses to the people as they needed it, fulfilling their spiritual desires during their forty years in the desert. And so it comes to us, as guidance every day.

Our goal is not merely to achieve a certain quantity of knowledge or a standard recipe for a good life. We want to use our minds to heal and realign ourselves with the Divine, to connect with our souls and with the very purpose for our existence. We want to use our minds to learn Torah. Learning Torah means not just reading the biblical text, but opening ourselves to receiving Divine guidance in our lives, guidance toward what is best for our growth and for the good of humanity. This kind of learning uses the power of human reason, but does not stop with rational analysis. Spiritual knowledge must be internalized in the whole person.

This is where Jewish mystical teachings about the mind are helpful. They teach that, to heal the mind, three powers must be functioning. To some extent, these powers are present in all mental work, but in normal life they are often not in balance. These are called *chochmah* or wisdom; *binah* or understanding; and *daat* or knowledge. Each helps in a different way to relate the mind to both the soul and the body.

The three can be portrayed in terms of right, left, and center brain functions, with *daat,* which is at the center, also connecting through the throat to the body below and outward toward knowledge of others.

Chochmah refers to the flash of inspiration that brings a new idea to a person, whether it be a scientific

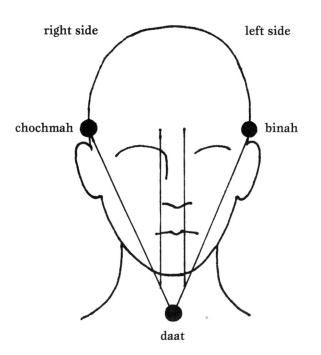

right side

left side

chochmah

binah

daat

or mathematical insight, or a fresh awareness of some feature of a friend's personality. A person suddenly sees things in a different way. We are rarely aware when this happens, for, unless the mind grasps and develops it, the new idea will disappear.

The *chochmah*-ability has its roots in the higher levels of the soul, and is largely unconscious. One way of interpreting *chochmah* is by rewriting the letters as *koach mah,* which literally means, "power of what?" In other words, it is the power of the unknown and inaccessible. Because of its unconscious connections, it is difficult to develop *chochmah* directly. We can, however, develop qualities that help us to be more receptive to inspiration and less desirous of dominating the world. Old-fashioned virtues such as humility, faith, and trust are excellent companions to *chochmah.*

As we approach Torah learning, we need to become more receptive by learning to listen fully and deeply to others before questioning and criticizing. In our society, we often pride ourselves on intellectual critique and being able to show the flaws in others' views. (If you doubt this, just read the editorial page of a newspaper or listen to a talk show.) Rarely are we encouraged to approach new thoughts with an accepting and trusting mind. But this is precisely what we need to receive Torah. Not that we won't question—the Jewish tradition is famous *for* questioning. But questioning must come from an attitude that the other person has something significant to say. So we must try first to understand completely what we are learning—what a textual passage really means, what the lecturer is trying to teach us in a class.

When we do this, two things happen. First, as psychology tells us, we are in better position to communicate authentically because we have tried to set aside our ego, at least for a short while, and truly "listen" to the text or the teacher. Second, and more deeply, we are better able to be aware of any "flash" of enlightening thought that is awakened in our own mind—the power of What? as it arises.

Binah is the power of mind by which an idea is nourished, developed, and related to other ideas. It is what we usually call thought, in the sense that thought is a process rather than a simple idea. *Binah* is on the "feminine" side of our natures, for it is like the womb in which a fetus develops until it is ready to come forth into the world. A thought can also be "in the back of our minds," as we say, a long time before it becomes fully conscious.

The Power of Thought

It sometimes happens that the spirit falls into depression, and the person cannot find any contentment, because he feels the paucity of his good deeds, because of an awareness of his misdeeds and his little diligence in the study of Torah. Such a person should concentrate on the secret potency of thought, realizing that "one who can infer one thing from another—his thought is more highly esteemed by the Holy One Blessed be He than all the sacrifices and burnt offerings." Holy thoughts and higher conceptual images therefore have all the efficacy of sacrifices, with all the rights pertaining to them.

...Therefore let him concentrate on the perception that the mending of the entire world and the healing of all souls depend on the basics of thought, and let him raise his thoughts to higher realms, to whatever extent he can, and he will reach a level of *teshuvah* out of love.

—*Rabbi Abraham Isaac Kook,* **The Lights of Penitence**[2]

This power can be consciously developed, through training in rational, analytical, mathematical, and logical processes as well as by the synthesizing processes of writing, developing speaking abilities, and artistic creation—in short, all kinds of training that allow one to develop creative and well-grounded thought. Jewish education offers this because it involves not only logic and rational thinking, but also metaphorical, poetic, and symbolic thinking, rich with stories, parables, and song.

How much study do we need? Since this is our "manna," it's like asking how much (spiritual) food we need. The prescription is: Different amounts for different people, regularly and, if possible, daily. The Sages ordained that the Torah must be read in public three times a week on Monday, Thursday, and Shabbat. Going three days without some Torah learning would be like fasting for seventy-two hours! Of course, hearing the Torah read aloud in synagogue is, for most of us, a rather cursory exposure to Torah. As we become more serious about healing our minds, we yearn for deeper learning. Most importantly, any Torah study is not mental gymnastics for its own sake, but is a step in a three-part process of the mind, culminating in inner transformation.

The stage of inner transformation develops with the third mental power, *daat,* "knowledge," through which thought is assimilated and comes to realization, making it truly *our* thought. *Daat* is the word used in the story of Creation for intimate knowing, as in "Adam knew his wife" (Genesis 4:1). For us, *daat* refers to the process whereby we reflect on our learning and connect our thoughts with the rest of our personality, including our previous knowledge and our emotions, behavior patterns, and physical health. Physically, *daat* is located in the central area of the face, from the midpoint between the eyes down to the throat. It is a channel through which thoughts come to be voiced. This includes not only the speech which is uttered through the mouth, expressing an intimate connection with the world by naming and using words, but also the inner voice that connects mind and heart.

One very important form of this inner voice is prayer.[3] With prayer, we can achieve the true and ultimate goal of study and mind-work: To "know God's name." This means, to become radiant with true Godliness so that "all the earth may be filled with the knowledge of God."

Balancing Mind and Body

How does this three-part mind enable us to integrate and balance the various parts of ourselves? How does thought heal?

Scientists have not yet been able to describe precisely how "thought" arises from the brain's chemical activity or how thoughts translate into actual behavior. Moreover, while it has long been an axiom of popular belief that a "will to live" is important in recovery from serious illness, science has not yet described exactly what that "will" is. Nevertheless, recent research has shown that a certain kind of thought does help the healing process—the kind of thought-and-speech that is called "prayer." In Judaism, prayer has been recommended for millennia as a path to healing and growth. The power of prayer is essential to understanding the relationship between body and soul and thus to the very concept of health. Prayer is the expression of the energy of *daat,* knowledge and awareness used for personal transformation.[4]

The wondrous organ of the mouth—its tongue, palate, teeth, and vocal cords—allows us to manifest, through speech, the creative energy given us by God. Just as God created the world by speaking, we also participate in the ongoing act of creation through speech. Yet, since we give the "first" of everything to God, the first and most important power of the mouth is to sing back to the Creator who gave us this gift: To praise and pray. It is our response to the special kind of learning we achieve through Torah study, for, as the great Hasidic scholar Rabbi Schneur Zalman of Liadi taught, Torah is "from above downward," while prayer is the service of man "from below upward."[5] We pray to rise toward God, to become our higher selves. At the same time, prayer reminds us that there is a power higher than ourselves.

Prayer is really our way of singing ourselves into existence before God. The Talmud describes it as an *avodah,* as labor, service, or work: "'You shall serve the Lord your God with all your heart' (Deut. 11:13). How does one serve with the heart? By praying" (*Taanit* 2a). But it is a different sort of work from our everyday occupations, since it is work on oneself, a kind of spiritual workout. The word *tefillah* (prayer) comes from the verb *pallel,* to judge, specifically from the form *l'hitpallel* which means to judge oneself. This suggests that prayer is a time of self-evaluation. Yet it is above all a healing process, not a lecturing to ourselves. We chant, sing, and sway, using the words of inspired poetry handed down through the ages, in order to cleanse away the old and make way for the new. It is a work of using the mind to look into the heart, placing ourselves in a closer union with God; it is a time to become aware of love, awe, trust, and faith.

The Torah tradition stipulates three times a day for prayer—*shacharit, mincha,* and *maariv* (morning, afternoon, and evening). *Halachah* (Jewish law) states that one should understand the words one is saying, so we are permitted to pray in any language. But learning to read Hebrew is universally recommended because, when one prays in Hebrew, one begins to understand the nuances of the prayers, and the Hebrew words resonate with one another in ways that cannot be communicated in English.[6] But, whether in English or Hebrew, we can set aside time each day to pray, expanding, little by little, our repertoire of prayers.

Like the Simple Son, we can learn with openness. When we add a prayer to our repertoire, we add to the creation of the world, for we build a spiritual edifice. Rabbi Nachman taught, "Every prayer that each individual prays represents a limb of the *Shekhinah* [Divine Presence].

These limbs correspond to the sections of the Tabernacle."[7] Indeed, some of the Psalms begin, "Sing to the Lord a New Song!"—for our new songs, or new singing of old songs, transform our very being.

Generally, one should pray aloud, or at least loud enough so that you can hear your own words. But the "silent" devotion of the *Shemoneh Esreh*—the standing prayer that is the centerpiece of the formal service—should be said very quietly to avoid disturbing others.

Hasidic traditions speak of some of the Rebbes using silent meditation or saying prayers inaudibly. Rabbi Nachman, on the other hand, suggested that one try praying in a loud, powerful voice and even clapping while praying. He taught that this produces, on the bodily level, "thunder," which comes from *gevurah* or strength (as in the blessing for thunder, "Blessed are you, Lord our God, Ruler of the universe, whose power and might *(gevurah)* fill the world"):

> When a person releases his voice with great force, his voice then strikes the "rain clouds"—which symbolize the mind—from where drop after drop descends. As is brought in the *Zohar* (III 235b) ..."'A well of living waters, and drops from Levanon' (Song of Songs 4.15): from the *LeVoNa,* the white of the mind."[8]

This alludes mystically to the convection current within clouds during a thunderstorm, which is the electrical current that we see as lightning. Rabbi Nachman's teaching suggests that we can use an analogous process to produce spiritual effects on our hearts, bringing balance and contentment by using a powerful voice in prayer.

Another important piece of advice from the sages is that we should talk to God. Whether we can pray formal prayers in Hebrew or not, we should set aside a time for, literally, a conversation with God—in seclusion, with no interruptions, and on a daily basis. This can be a powerful way to awaken *daat,* the process of internalizing our understanding.

All these guidelines make it clear that prayer must become our own spiritual expression. Reciting words by rote is not prayer. True prayer contains our heart's desire to rise up to God. As a Hasidic master once said, "Do not think that the words of prayer as you say them go up to God; it is not the words themselves that ascend, it is rather the burning desire of your heart that rises like smoke to heaven."[9] Only in this way can we truly realize our higher selves.

Although it may sound like work, prayer is also exciting, stimulating, and joyful. Above all, the Sages say, one should make every effort to arouse joy in prayer. Arousing ourselves to joy is the work of *daat*. It is a dance that links mind, body, and emotions and is designed to bring them into harmony.

When we learn to pray, we sing our own song and express our unique joy in living. Then we have a wholeness of mind, and we begin to create the whole person that God wants us to be, for as the commandment says, "Take the utmost care of your vital souls" (Deuteronomy 4:9).

Now that we are aware of the importance of prayer, we can return to our morning blessings. After the blessings over the Torah, we add passages from the Torah, then follow these with a short meditation.

Creating a New Mind: Movement and Meditation

You may sit or stand. Place both thumbs under your chin near the center. Place your two index fingers on either side of the bridge of your nose, close to your eyes. Press your fingers into these points, and let your head rest on them. Your head will be tipped forward and remain in this position throughout the prayer. (You are applying pressure to points that stimulate the brain.) Then read the "Selections from the Torah" beginning, "May the Lord bless you and safeguard you" (we present them here only in English). Continue with the meditation that follows.

בָּרוּךְ אַתָּה, יְיָ אֱלֹהֵינוּ, מֶלֶךְ הָעוֹלָם, אֲשֶׁר קִדְּשָׁנוּ בְּמִצְוֹתָיו
וְצִוָּנוּ לַעֲסוֹק בְּדִבְרֵי תוֹרָה. וְהַעֲרֶב-נָא, יהוה אֱלֹהֵינוּ, אֶת-דִּבְרֵי
תוֹרָתְךָ בְּפִינוּ, וּבְפִי עַמְּךָ בֵּית יִשְׂרָאֵל, וְנִהְיֶה אֲנַחְנוּ וְצֶאֱצָאֵינוּ,
וְצֶאֱצָאֵי עַמְּךָ בֵּית יִשְׂרָאֵל, כֻּלָּנוּ יוֹדְעֵי שְׁמֶךָ וְלוֹמְדֵי תוֹרָתֶךָ
לִשְׁמָהּ. בָּרוּךְ אַתָּה, יהוה, הַמְלַמֵּד תּוֹרָה לְעַמּוֹ יִשְׂרָאֵל.

בָּרוּךְ אַתָּה, יהוה, אֱלֹהֵינוּ מֶלֶךְ הָעוֹלָם, אֲשֶׁר בָּחַר בָּנוּ מִכָּל
הָעַמִּים, וְנָתַן לָנוּ אֶת תּוֹרָתוֹ. בָּרוּךְ אַתָּה, יהוה, נוֹתֵן הַתּוֹרָה.

Ba-ruch a-ta, A-do-nai, El-o-he-nu, Me-lech ha-olam, a-sher kid'sha-nu b'mitz-vo-tav, v'tzi-va-nu la-a-sok b'di-vrei To-rah.
V'ha-a-rev-na, A-do-nai El-o-he-nu, et di-vrei to-rat'cha b'fi-nu, u-v'fi am'cha beit Yis-ra-el. V'ni-yeh a-nach-nu v'tze-tza-e-nu v'tze-tza-ei am'cha beit Yis-ra-el, ku-la-nu yo-dei sh'me-cha v'lom-dei to-ra-te-cha lish-mah. Ba-ruch a-ta, A-do-nai, ham-la-med To-rah l'a-mo Yis-ra-el.
Ba-ruch a-ta, A-do-nai, El-o-he-nu Me-lech ha-olam, a-sher ba-char ba-nu mi-kal ha-a-mim, v'na-tan la-nu et To-ra-to. Ba-ruch a-ta, A-do-nai, no-ten ha-To-rah.

Blessed are You, Adonai, our God, Ruler of the universe, who has sanctified us with Your commandments and commanded us to be absorbed in words of Torah.
Please, Adonai our God, make the words of Your Torah pleasant in our mouths, and in the mouth of Your people the House of Israel. May it be that we and our offspring and the offspring of Your people the House of Israel, all of us, know Your Name and study Your Torah for its own sake. Blessed are You, Adonai, the Teacher of Torah to Your people Israel.
Blessed are You, Adonai our God, Ruler of the universe, who chooses us from all peoples and gives us Your Torah. Blessed are You, who gives the Torah.

Selections from the Torah

May the Lord bless you and safeguard you. May the Lord's face shine upon you and be gracious to you. May the Lord's face be turned toward you and give you peace. (Numbers 6:24-26)

These are the things that have no prescribed measure: the corner of a field [that must be left for the poor], the first-fruit offering, pilgrimage [to Jerusalem], acts of kindness, and Torah study. (Mishnah *Peah* 1:1)

These are the things whose fruits a person enjoys in this world, and the principal remains for him in the World to Come. They are: honoring father and mother, acts of kindness, coming early to the house of study morning and evening, hospitality to guests, visiting the sick, providing for a bride, escorting the dead, absorption in prayer, bringing peace between one human being and another—and the study of Torah is equivalent to them all. (Talmud, *Shabbat* 127a)

Meditation

Take a deep breath. Visualize the mind as a kiddush *cup that holds a little wine from the night before. Tilt your head front, right, and left, imagining your mind emptying as the* kiddush *cup spills its old wine. Breathe deeply in and out.*

Lift your head gently. Visualize a crystal decanter over your head, filled with the finest wine. Imagine the wine turning into the shapes of letters and filling the cup inside your head with the wisdom of holy words.

Now imagine the taste of the wine on your lips, and savor its delicious flavor. Imagine yourself with your family or friends, sharing it with everyone you know.

See the fine wine as Torah, and let it fill your mind, pushing out needless chatter, negative voices, pointless arguments and painful exchanges. Focus on your mind filling with the shower of sweetness that is God's light.

Take a deep breath and exhale, with a sound. Open your mouth and be aware of its potential for goodness, thanksgiving, and song. Thank God for teaching us Torah and for choosing us to house this beauty.

אֱלֹהַי, נְשָׁמָה שֶׁנָּתַתָּ בִּי טְהוֹרָה הִיא. אַתָּה בְרָאתָהּ,
אַתָּה יְצַרְתָּהּ, אַתָּה נְפַחְתָּהּ בִּי, וְאַתָּה מְשַׁמְּרָהּ בְּקִרְבִּי.
וְאַתָּה עָתִיד לִטְּלָהּ מִמֶּנִּי, וּלְהַחֲזִירָהּ בִּי לֶעָתִיד לָבֹא.
כָּל־זְמַן שֶׁהַנְּשָׁמָה בְּקִרְבִּי, מוֹדֶה אֲנִי לְפָנֶיךָ, יהוה אֱלֹהַי
וֵאלֹהֵי אֲבוֹתַי, רִבּוֹן כָּל־הַמַּעֲשִׂים, אֲדוֹן כָּל־הַנְּשָׁמוֹת.
בָּרוּךְ אַתָּה, יהוה, הַמַּחֲזִיר נְשָׁמוֹת לִפְגָרִים מֵתִים.

My God, the soul that You have placed in me is pure! You created it, You formed it, You breathed it into me. You safeguard it
within me, and eventually You will take it from me and restore
it to me in time to come. As long as the soul is within me, I
gratefully thank You, Adonai, my God and the God of my ancestors, Master of all works, Lord of all souls. Blessed are You,
Adonai, who restores souls to dead bodies.

To practice the prayer with its movement and meditation, please turn to page 119.

5
Connecting with the Soul

LET'S RETURN TO waking up in the morning. The body may want to remain in bed, and the mind may be revving up for its constant daily chatter, but the soul has just re-entered the scene.

At night, the soul's ties to the body are loosened, and it can travel beyond space and time. Since, as the Talmud says, "sleep is one-sixtieth of death," sometimes the soul can connect with the realm of souls or angels. Because "dreams are one-sixtieth of prophecy" (*Berachot* 57b), occasionally the soul can pick up actual information about the past or future, or about things happening in other locations. Sometimes, the soul is integrating information from deeply-buried files of the mind of which we are usually unaware. Sometimes it is simply trying to heal the heart by processing emotional difficulties from the previous days. What is remembered from our dreams is usually not in linear or rational form, because linear thinking was inactive while we were sleeping. That is why dreams are usually symbolic and difficult to understand.[1]

In any case, upon coming back into full union with the body, the soul again assumes the limits of this world of form. This goes against its essential nature which, the Jewish mystical tradition tells us, is to ascend to God as the flame of a candle rises upward, and to unite with its Divine Source.[2] But God has given the soul a mission, and the soul returns each morning to perform it. We respond by giving thanks: a special blessing for the soul.

El-o-hai... The blessing over the soul begins intimately, not with "Lord our God, Ruler of the Universe," but with "Elohai," *my* God. This prayer expresses personal gratitude for the divine source of the soul, and strengthens us for the tasks of life.

Ne-sha-ma she-na-ta-ta bi, t'ho-rah hi, "The soul that You have placed in me is pure." Judaism conceives of the soul as "pure," as distinguished from other faiths which speak of an "original sin" that corrupts the human soul. According to Jewish teachings, the soul cannot be contaminated. The essential soul has a source beyond the limits of space-time, so that *teshuvah,* "return" to God, is always possible.[3] Its purity is analogous to the freshness of each new day when we have the possibility of fresh intentions and a good will.

A-ta v'ra-tah, a-ta ye-zar-ta, a-ta n'fach-ta bi, "You created it, You formed it, You breathed it into me," refers to the levels or "descents" of the soul through the Four Worlds described in Kabbalah. The world of Emanation *(Atzilut)* is the world of purity and direct connection to God. The world of Creation *(Beriah)* is the level where the elements of the created world are conceived by God, and from which human souls originate. In the world of Formation *(Yetzirah),* the energetic qualities emerge that will determine the form of an entity. Finally, the world of Action *(Asiyah)* is the material world as we perceive it. There, the soul is united with the body.[4] We can conceive this process according to the chart at the top of the next page.

V'a-ta m'sham-ra b'kir-bi, "You safeguard it within me." God guards the soul, and will not let it escape from the body. But God restrains the soul, because God wants it to enlighten the body.

V'a-ta a-tid lit-la mi-me-ni, "Eventually You will take it from me" refers to the time when the dead will be resurrected.

Kal z'man she-ha-ne-sha-ma v'kir-bi, mo-deh a-ni l'fa-ne-cha, "As long as the soul is within me, I gratefully thank You." Our purpose in life is to connect the earthly body with the Divine. One of the ways we do this is to thank God, for in a sense, our prayers help keep the soul in the body,

אצילות *Atzilut* Emanation	*t'ho·rah hi:* "the soul is pure" and connected to God
בראיה *Beriah* Creation	*A·ta v'ra·tah:* "You created it" in thought
יצירה *Yetzirah* Formation	*a·ta ye·tzar·ta:* "You formed it" and gave it an identity
עשיה *Asiyah* Action	*a·ta n'fach·ta bi:* "You breathed it into me."

sending an internal message to the soul that we are ready and willing to cooperate in the purpose of life.

This phrase also expresses our trust that we will awaken each day. Our daily reawakening hints at the resurrection of the body in the "world to come," and at the end of the blessing we thank God as the One who restores life to the dead: *ha-ma-cha-zir ne-sha-mot lif-ga-rim me-tim*. In the meantime, we praise God each day for our renewed life in this world.

Just as the Holy One, blessed be He, fills the whole world, so the soul fills the body.

Just as the Holy One, blessed be He, sees but is not seen, so the soul sees but is not itself seen.

Just as the Holy One, blessed be He, feeds the whole world, so the soul feeds the whole body.

Just as the Holy One, blessed be He, is pure, so the soul is pure.

Just as the Holy One, blessed be He, dwells in the innermost chamber of chambers, so the soul dwells in the innermost chamber of chambers.

Let that which has these five qualities come and praise Him who has these five qualities.

—*Talmud Bavli*, **Berachot 10a**

The Soul and the Purpose of Life

When we say the blessing over the soul, we are not just thanking God for life, but for additional *levels* of life. The transcendent soul gives us a life that is more than just instinct, habit, and social forms. The soul takes on bodily form for a specific, higher purpose because it possesses the knowledge about why we are here and what tools we have for accomplishing our spiritual goals.

Deep down, we know that we aren't here merely to accumulate money, possessions, or pleasurable experiences. We are here to grow and develop spiritually, and to help others evolve (including animals, plants, and the earth itself). That is the meaning of the famous teaching of "the Holy Ari," Isaac Luria, that we are to "raise the sparks" of holiness that have fallen in a broken world. Because we carry this inner knowledge of a higher purpose, most of us become restless at a certain point in our life, hungry for something beyond the "rat race" of freeways and money-making, beyond the dulling influences of television and advertising. We may find ourselves unhappy, or victims of an addiction, or just plain bored with life. Such signals tell us that we're ready to find a new and more meaningful level of existence, ready to explore the levels of the soul and find out what it has to teach us.

Jewish tradition, whether in the philosophical and contemplative style of the Rambam or the passionate mysticism of Luria, has been telling us for a long time to be in touch with our souls.[5] But during the past two centuries, rationalism has held most of us in its grip, making it hard even to believe in the existence of the soul, let alone listen to it. Now, the cultural milieu is changing, and more people are ready to listen. Substantial research has developed on "out-of-the-body" experiences, such as the work on near-death experiences reported in the 1970s by Dr. Raymond Moody. Those who have had these experiences often find that they care more about others than they did before, and that they have a greater sense of purpose and destiny in life.[6]

One Israeli who experienced near-death was Rachel Noam, a young woman raised on a secular kibbutz, who was walking down the street when a heavy beam fell on her head from five stories up. Such a blow should have been fatal. Instead, she found herself separating from her body, and looking down on it from above. She was drawn toward a loving, brilliant light and saw the events of her life streaking before her eyes. Feeling herself melting into and bonding with the presence, she asked to be returned to her body and be given another chance on earth. Her request was granted. She returned to her body, got up, and was assisted to go home. She suffered migraine headaches for some time, but was otherwise unhurt. Doctors could not explain her survival. Nevertheless, the experience convinced her that her previous life had been inconsequential, and she began a quest to rediscover Jewish spirituality.[7]

New research has also appeared on reincarnation, including detailed historical research as well as reliable psychiatrists' reports of patients under hypnosis.[8] These reports confirm what Jewish mystics have taught: Souls may incarnate more than once, and every soul is on a journey of learning, growing, and spiritual refinement that may take many lifetimes. The great eighteenth-century scholar, Rabbi Moshe Chaim Luzzatto, stated the principle of reincarnation: "A single soul can be reincarnated a number of times in different bodies, and in this manner, it can rectify the damage done in previous incarnations. Similarly, it can also achieve perfection that was not attained in its previous incarnations."[9]

Yet, Jewish tradition does not encourage us to focus on learning about our various incarnations. God has given us Yom Kippur, the day each year when we look at how we have lived our life—just as souls review the entirety of their lives after death. We can wipe the slate clean and "choose life" every year. We just need to listen to the voice of our soul.

The rivulets of the supernal life of the pure soul run in the depths, in the depths of bodily nature; in the nethermost of flesh and blood they churn and groan.
  And yet they crash upward, shrieking and crying, undulating and grumbling, striving, twisting ceaselessly to reach the height, that there may be revealed in a luminous form whole life, full of splendor, majesty, and the glory, the beauty of the strength of the most holy.

Happy is the man who hears the voice of his soul from his depths;
happy is the people that hears the reverberation of its universal soul, how it rocks from its depths;
happy is the pure listener who hears the echo of all creation calling from its depths for sublime, pure, holy revelation.

—*from Rav Abraham Isaac Kook*, Orot *(1920)*[10]

Maps of the Soul

Just as we turned our microscope on the regions of the body and the workings of the mind, so we need to look more closely at the various dimensions of the soul. After all, the soul holds the key to understanding our purpose for being on earth, so it is worthwhile to try to listen to its vibrations.

We mentioned in earlier chapters that there are various words for the soul, and that the *nefesh* or vital soul is connected to the blood, while the *ruach* or spirit is related to the breath. Each of these words refers to the soul's energy as it has intertwined with the human body in a particular way. *Nefesh* is usually identified with the lower torso, and appears to correspond to *ch'i* or *ki* in Chinese and Japanese traditions, respectively. *Ruach,* as we saw in our discussion of the upper torso, is usually identified with the emotional center.

Another word frequently used is *neshamah,* which is related to *nishmat,* a word for breath. Often *neshamah* is used as the most general term for the person's unique soul, manifest in the personality, so that a person might say, "She has such a beautiful *neshamah.*" Sometimes *neshamah* refers specifically to the mental level of the soul. We will normally use it in this latter way. The term indicates the highest level we can normally experience, and it has more to do with the intellectual level, the "mental body," than with the emotional or physical.

Less familiar terms refer to two additional levels of the soul, *chaya* and *yechida. Chaya* (literally, "living one") is the level of the soul as it first enters the personality. *Yechida* ("unique one") is the soul in its essence, a spark of God with a unique purpose or "will to be." We are rarely aware of *chaya,* and almost never of *yechida,* though they are constantly present. We cannot be aware of anything unless it comes through our bodily apparatus in some way, at least through some kind of electrical influence in our nervous system. In the accompanying diagram, these latter two are shown as "surrounding" influences, not part of the physical system. The three lower levels of the soul are represented as intertwining with the body in different kinds of energies.

The levels of mental, emotional, and physical aspects of the soul are articulated further by the system of *sefirot.* The mystical tradition teaches that the whole of Creation unfolded according to a gradual, sequential manifestation of Divine energies through the Four Worlds mentioned above. The *sefirot* are the map of God's energy-manifestation (but not of the Divine Essence, which can never be known completely). Since everything in creation unfolded from God, the *sefirot* are also part of every creation. Therefore, they are a map of the human being as well. To put it another way, the *sefirot* reveal the mystical patterns in common between the "microcosm," that is, the human being, and the "macrocosm," God-in-manifestation. In regard to the body, the *sefirot* do not offer an exact map of physical systems, though they loosely correspond to internal organs, functions, or limbs. We can more appropriately think of them as a system of energies.[11]

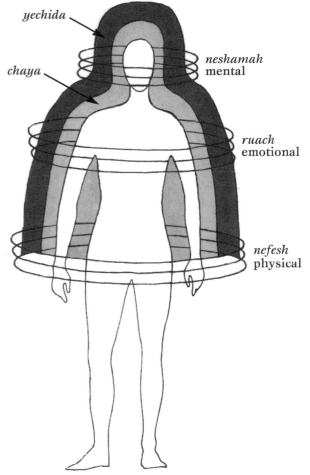

The *sefirot* are most often depicted as a "tree," a series of branches that form three principal triangles. (The tree, by the way, is upside-down: its roots are Above, in its Divine source, while its furthest branch is below, manifesting in the physical world.) The highest point represents the highest level of the soul, *yechida;* the corners of the highest triangle correspond to *chaya* and *neshamah.* The next triangle corresponds to *ruach,* while the lowest triangle plus the tenth *sefirah* corresponds to the *nefesh.* The accompanying diagram places all of these on the human body. The arrows represent the direction of energy.[12]

The system of *sefirot* is the best-known way of depicting the energies of the body as a reflection of the energies of the Divine, since we were created *b'tzelem Elohim,* in the image of God. That is why we have used the points of the *sefirot* to organize the regions of the body and to focus your meditations. Now we need to understand the specific powers they represent.

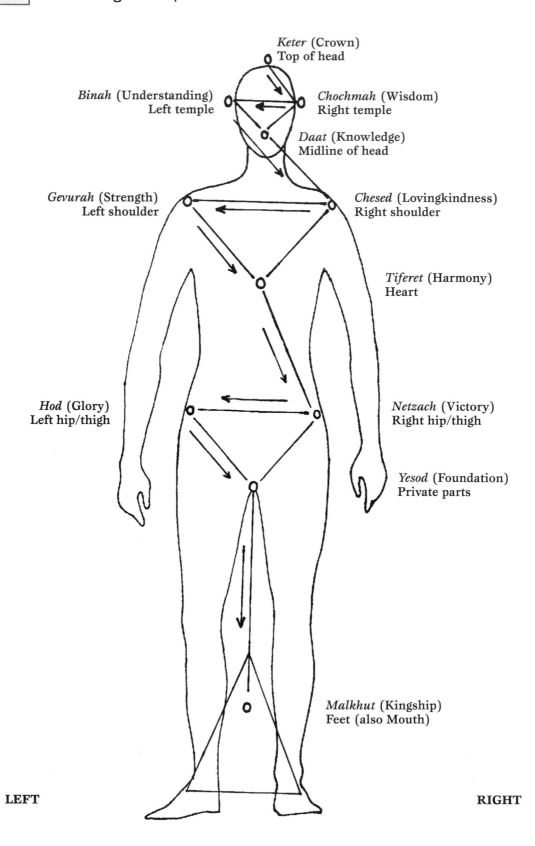

Keter (Crown)
Top of head

Binah (Understanding)
Left temple

Chochmah (Wisdom)
Right temple

Daat (Knowledge)
Midline of head

Gevurah (Strength)
Left shoulder

Chesed (Lovingkindness)
Right shoulder

Tiferet (Harmony)
Heart

Hod (Glory)
Left hip/thigh

Netzach (Victory)
Right hip/thigh

Yesod (Foundation)
Private parts

Malkhut (Kingship)
Feet (also Mouth)

LEFT

RIGHT

The *Sefirot*

In what follows, we will trace the path through the labyrinth of the soul as specifically as possible. These descriptions may seem abstract at first, but, as you try to apply them to your own life, they will gradually become a part of your self-understanding. We suggest that you make brief notes, daily if possible, in a "Journal of the *Sefirot*." An outline of such a journal appears on pages 115–118. Then, as you compare your notes with the descriptions here, you will begin to see how the qualities of your own soul manifest in your life.

☐ *Sefirot* of Will and Thought

Spiritual energy enters the field of the body at the Crown, *Keter,* through the area of the fontanel, the "soft spot" on an infant's skull. This is the fundamental, non-physical energy of Will. Kabbalah teaches that Will, or *ratzon,* is the most powerful force in the universe. The saying "Where there's a will, there's a way," echoes that sentiment, and our awareness of the power of "will" is reflected also in our knowledge that the "will to live" is a very important factor in healing.

On a spiritual level, Will is the force that brings the soul into a human incarnation to serve a higher purpose. This is sometimes expressed in the metaphor that the soul makes a "contract" to accomplish certain things on earth. If we are in touch with that original Will of our soul, it can guide everything that we do. In light of our overarching purpose, we can organize our priorities and manage our lives in efficient, meaningful, and satisfying ways.

Most of the time, however, our early education and social pressures cause us to bury our original knowledge of our purpose in life. As the colorful expression of the midrash puts it, we have an indentation above our upper lip because, just before we were born, an angel pressed its finger to our lips, "sealing" our knowledge inside. As a result, we are tempted to unite our wills with merely human or even animal purposes, pursuing material pleasures, power, or accomplishments. Getting in touch with our original spiritual Will can be a powerful tool to re-connect with our souls.

The energy flows from *Keter* into what are called the *Sefirot* of Thought. First it goes to *Chochmah,* Wisdom, which is also the *chaya* level of the soul. As we saw in the chapter on mind, *Chochmah* represents the center of inspiration, the "spark" of new ideas that seem to come from "nowhere." In reality, new spiritual thoughts continuously stream from the never-ending flow of divine creative energy that pours into the world. We are not aware of these new "ideas" coming into ourselves, because most of the time we are preoccupied with the material tasks before us. Part of the necessary equipment of being able to function in the world is the inherent ability to "screen out" even divine inspiration. This is why we are not normally aware of the soul level of *chaya,* which has its primary point of manifestation here. Sometimes, nevertheless, the sparks of new ideas come through dreams, or when our minds are relaxed after a long struggle of trying to solve a problem or understand something difficult. Sometimes, when we hear a voice whispering, "Try this!" or "Watch out!" we are catching just a quick flash of the supernal Will of our soul trying to turn us in the right direction.

The energy of the soul then travels through *Binah* and *Daat* which represent Understanding and Knowledge. Those thoughts that we accept, whether from our own inner awareness or from outside in the form of sense perceptions (images, impressions, sounds of other's words, words we read, etc.), then become "clothed," as Kabbalah says, in the energy of *Binah,* which is also the center of the *neshamah* level of the soul. *Binah* nourishes the divine spark just as a fetus is nourished in the womb. The integration of *Binah* and *Chochmah* takes place in the so-called "eleventh" *sefirah, Daat* or Knowledge, as an internalization of awareness. *Daat* is the transformational point, where the energy can move from one kind of power into another.

Chochmah and *Binah* are involved with Thought. They are analogous to the World of Creation, the second of the Four Worlds. At this level everything is still private, in the recesses of the mind. Even if a person has mentally planned a house, complete with every detail, it has never been manifested. In order for it to come into being at all, it has to be transferred from the *Sefirot* of Thought to the *Sefirot* of Building, the next six *sefirot.* Sometimes this transition is difficult. We cannot seem to follow through with our ideas, to allow ourselves to feel them deeply and be motivated to act. This is the problem of the "straits of the neck"—thoughts get stuck in the head, so to speak. *Daat* is the power to transform them, and that is why we associated *Daat* with prayer in the last chapter. Through prayer, one can open the channels of one's being and make inspiration become a lived reality.

☐ *Sefirot* of Emotions

The next six *sefirot,* the *Sefirot* of Building, are divided into two triangles of three each. Each *sefirah* at this level is connected with a *middah* or character trait. If you think of people you know who are extraordinary in certain modes of action, you may be able to see these traits exemplified. Here, we will describe them through outstanding masculine and feminine figures from biblical tradition. If you are not already familiar with the stories, consult the endnote for the biblical references so you can enjoy reading about them yourself.[13]

The first three, which have to do with emotions, are named *Chesed, Gevurah, Tiferet:* Lovingkindness, Discipline, and Harmony (also identified with Beauty or Truth). They are associated with the soul-level of *ruach,* centering in the heart.

Chesed is the energy of lovingkindness, which continually strives to be outgoing and giving. Traditionally, this *sefirah* is represented by the figure of Abraham. The story in the Bible that most exemplifies this trait is of Abraham sitting at the opening of his tent on a hot, sunny day, after having circumcised himself at God's command. He was experiencing a vision of God, when suddenly three travelers appeared on the road. Abraham, despite the pain in his body and his exalted spiritual state, jumped up, invited them to stop at his tent, then prepared a feast for them. It turned out that they were angels, but Abraham didn't know that. Ever after, Abraham became the prototype of *Chesed,* lovingkindness, in the form of hospitality beyond the call of duty. Even more important than experiencing a vision of God was his love for and desire to build relationships with people. As the Torah also tells us, he converted many people to the service of God through this love.

Ruth is also known for her *chesed.* Although born into a Moabite noble family, she had married a Jewish man whose family had come to live in Moab. Her husband, father-in-law, and brother-in-law all died, leaving her and her mother-in-law, Naomi, destitute. Despite the fact that she had no inheritance in Israel, tradition tells us that Ruth loved her mother-in-law and her Jewish customs so deeply that she returned to Israel with Naomi and converted to Judaism. She even humbled herself to gather the gleanings of the crops with the poor in order to provide for Naomi, and accepted a much older man as her husband in order to keep her ex-husband's family line alive and keep the property in the family for Naomi. The *chesed* of Ruth, Naomi, and Ruth's husband

Boaz, are so pervasive in this story that the Sages say that the Book of Ruth is all about *chesed.*

These figures represent the quality of *Chesed* at its finest: a quality of soul that led them to forsake personal pleasure for the sake of others. Yet it also needs to be balanced with inner strength and restraint. A person can love too much, like a parent who gives a child everything and does not use discipline, or a person who gives too much time to community activities and feels empty inside. The soul-quality of *Gevurah,* literally strength, manifests as discipline and restraint. The patriarch Isaac, who was much more inward-turning than his father, traditionally represents *Gevurah.* The Torah tells that he re-dug the wells of his father Abraham, which had been covered over. This suggests symbolically that he dug deeper into himself, and was not so concerned with reaching out to others. Isaac also underwent the trial of being bound for sacrifice (the *Akedah*), which made him very aware of his relationship to God. As a result of his once having been designated as a holy offering, God did not allow him to leave the land of Israel. This too suggests the boundaries and restraint that are associated with *Gevurah.*

Biblical figures such as Devorah and Huldah also suggest elements of *gevurah.* Devorah was a judge and prophetess in the period after the Jewish people returned to Israel after their slavery in Egypt. She had to gather the people for war, discipline them, and forge a strong army by virtue of her spiritual power. Huldah, a prophetess centuries later during the kingship of Josiah, warned the king that he had to follow the laws set out in the Torah, in the book of laws that had been rediscovered, or face severe consequences from God. She embodied the energy of strictness, demanding that the people and even the king observe boundaries and self-restraint.

The third of the *sefirot* of emotions is *Tiferet* or harmony. Some associate it also with *Emet* or truth. As the Divine energy flows between *Chesed* and *Gevurah,* it ultimately finds a balance in *Tiferet.* Jacob, the third of the patriarchs, represents the integration of his father and grandfather in this respect. By balancing inward-seeking and outgoing qualities, he became a "simple" person, as the Torah tells us, who was happy to sit in his tent, in harmony with his own inner truth, while his twin brother, Esau, became a hunter and later a warrior. Jacob was able to maintain his simplicity, even though he became quite wealthy while serving his uncle Laban (in return for marrying Laban's two daughters). Because of his balanced personality and complete faith in God, he was able to withstand the loss of his beloved wife, Rachel; disputes with his neighbors; and difficulties with his sons, even the disappearance of his beloved son Joseph for more than twenty years. His twelve sons each became the head of a tribe among the Jewish people. The whole nation was named after him: Israel. Jacob, like *Tiferet,* represents the heart center and therefore the integration of will, intellect, and emotion in love and awe of God.

Among the women of the Bible, Sarah represents *Tiferet* very clearly, as beauty, harmony, and truth. The Torah tells us that she was beautiful, wise, and spiritually powerful. She also experienced ecstatic joy at the birth of her son Isaac when she was ninety years old. However, she had to come to a balance of *chesed* and *gevurah* in a striking way. Because she was childless, she gave her handmaid, Hagar, to Abraham as a concubine. We can understand this as an act of *chesed* to him. Later, however, after Sarah became pregnant and bore their son Isaac, she perceived that Hagar's son, Ishmael, was not a good influence. Abraham, a man of *chesed,* wanted to keep him in the family but Sarah recognized that *gevurah* had to come into play. She insisted that Hagar and Ishmael leave (Genesis 21:9-10). From the point of view of the development of the soul, harmony could emerge only if discipline were exercised.

These three *sefirot* represent the interplay of motives, emotional desires and impulses that are most characteristic of a person. Through contemplation of these qualities, we can identify the natural tendencies of our soul and live them fully, while also learning to balance and integrate them in light of our higher purpose. The deeper our understanding of our emotional drives, the better we will be able to allow the spiritual energy to flow smoothly into all the channels.

☐ *Sefirot* of Action

The second triangle of the *Sefirot* of Building alludes to the instinctual and physical body, represented by *Netzach, Hod, Yesod*: Victory, Glory, Foundation. *Netzach* and *Hod* are almost always treated as a pair, for they are closely related as a source of vital energy located at the navel center (and corresponding to *ch'i* or *ki* in Chinese and Japanese medicine and martial arts). On the map of the body, they are associated with the hips, thighs, and the movement of the legs. *Netzach* is like the right leg stepping forward. It suggests perseverance, or a continuing forward movement. *Hod* is the left leg coming to stabilize. It represents standing in alignment, containing energy, and balancing. The word *hod* is also related to *todah* or thanksgiving, and its literal meaning is "glory." This suggests that when we are in physical balance, we are in position to actively appreciate and "glorify" the world and its Maker. In addition, the thighs, which are the strongest muscles in our bodies, provide our principal physical support. Thus *Netzach* and *Hod* also represent material resources and money—our worldly "support."

Netzach, the energy of motion, initiative, and perseverance, is represented by Moses, the greatest leader in Jewish history. Moses confronted Pharaoh, led the Israelites out of Egypt and through the Red Sea, and took them to Mount Sinai. An unequivocal example of his manifesting the soul-quality of perseverance occurred when the people were confronted with a desperate battle against the tribe of Amalek. Moses held his arms up in the sky and, as long as he did so, the people had courage to continue. When his arms became tired, Joshua and Aaron held them up, until the Israelites were finally victorious. As the books of Exodus, Leviticus, Numbers and Deuteronomy tell us, Moses persevered for forty years, despite the people's complaints, criticism, and near-mutiny, always urging them to move onward and upward, spiritually as well as physically, until they could come into the Land as a pure and holy people.

Among women, Miriam, Moses' sister, also represents *Netzach*. She urged her father not to give up during the period of slavery, to re-marry his wife and to continue having children. During the Exodus, she was leader of the women, singing inspired songs after the crossing of the Sea. And because of her, the Israelites had a well of water through all their travels in the desert.

Aaron, the High Priest, represents *Hod,* the container or balancing force. Aaron was the master of ceremony, who led the people in thanking and glorifying God. The place of worship, the *Mishkan,* was a stabilizing force in the midst of the people's movement through the desert. The prayers and sacrifices kept the people oriented "vertically" in relationship to God. Moreover, Aaron was known as the peacemaker, a stabilizing force in the community. According to the midrash, when he heard that two people were in conflict, he would go to one of them and say, "Your friend really wants to make peace, why don't you talk to him?" Then he would go to the other and say, "It seems to me that so-

and-so really feels sorry that he got into an argument with you. Maybe it's time to make peace." He did the same with husband and wife. In this way, he elicited the goodness in everyone.

Among women, one of King David's wives, Abigail, represented the quality of *Hod*. Before David was king of Israel, he was hiding with his band of men, trying to elude King Saul, who wanted to kill him. David's men protected the people of the countryside from marauders. In return, he asked for their support by way of food and supplies. Once, he sent a message to a wealthy man, asking him for support. The man sneered and refused. This was Abigail's husband. David thought this might undermine his support among the populace, and he prepared to teach the man a lesson by taking revenge. When Abigail heard what her husband had done, she secretly took a caravan laden with food and supplies to David. God rewarded her with the gift of prophecy, and she was able to foretell David's future kingship. Shortly afterward, her husband died of natural (or supernatural) causes, and David took her as a wife. Abigail knew how to express thanksgiving and peacemaking in one grand gesture, thus embodying the energy of *Hod*.

These mobilizing forces are combined and channeled into the creative energy of *Yesod,* which is associated with Joseph. As a boy, Joseph received from his father a "coat of many colors," which according to mystical tradition symbolized the various *sefirot* that would be channeled through him, for *Yesod* is the channel for all the *sefirot* above it. He contained within himself great forces of passion (as signified by the location of *Yesod* at the sexual organs). In the Torah's account of Joseph's life, he was sold into slavery, then earned a position of great responsibility in the house of his owner. But he faced a great temptation from his owner's wife, who found him extremely attractive. At the crucial moment, the midrash says, the face of his father appeared to him, and Joseph was able to resist her. Mystically, this means that Joseph's quality of *yesod* was directly connected to the "heart," *Tiferet,* which is associated with Jacob. Joseph thus integrated the energies of the "central pillar" of the tree of the *sefirot,* channeling all the spiritual energy from above into the force of his passions, but purifying them and turning them to Godly purposes.

Another figure who represents this *sefirah* is Boaz, the husband of Ruth. As part of Naomi's plan to marry off Ruth, she sent her to Boaz's threshing floor on the night of the harvest celebration. Boaz had already shown kindness to Ruth by taking her under his protection during the harvest, but nothing more. To his surprise, Ruth offered herself to him. Boaz, however, recognized that the family had a closer relative than he who had the right to marry Ruth. So, despite the obvious opportunity to take advantage of Ruth, he told her that he could not yet marry her. Boaz's self-control reflects his character. He had already shown her great *chesed,* and now he showed that he was a man of action, taking the steps to ensure her full acceptance in the community. All his qualities flowed through *Yesod* and made him the "redeemer" who had the merit of being a direct ancestor of King David.

Among women, Tamar and Judith exemplified the soul-quality of *Yesod.* Tamar was a priest's daughter married to one of the sons of Judah (Jacob and Leah's fourth son). When he died, she married another of his sons, but he also died. Judah did not want to marry her to his third son, even though tradition required it, because he feared the deaths of his first two sons were her fault. She disguised herself as a harlot, enticed Judah, and became pregnant. Later, when he found out his daughter-in-law was pregnant, he was about to have her burned, but she proved he was the father. "She is more righteous than I," Judah proclaimed, and accepted her as a wife. One of the twins born to them was an ancestor of King David.

Judith was an extremely devout widow living in seclusion in a town near Jerusalem. When the nation was under threat from an army from the north, Judith transformed herself into a beautiful woman, secretly went to the enemy camp, and gained entry into the tent of the general by allowing him to believe he might seduce her. After she plied him with wine, he fell asleep, and she killed him. This demoralized the enemy, and her heroic act saved the nation from conquerors for many years.

Both these women took unusual steps in channeling the passion of sexuality for the benefit of the Jewish people—in Tamar's case, to preserve Judah's special lineage, destined to lead to the Messiah; with Judith, to save the Jews from physical destruction. The lineage from Judah to David suggests the channeling of energy into a powerful creative force, while the routing of the enemy represents removal of evil and a return to purity. When *Yesod* manifests, a great force of passion must be channeled and controlled. If we are successful, the *kelipot* or "husks" of evil are shattered and the light shines through.

□ *Sefirah* of Receptivity and Transformation

All the spiritual energies of the soul, when illuminated, flow into *Malkhut,* our complete manifestation in the "world of action," the world of *Asiyah* in which we are material entities. This force is embodied in our feet that go forth to do God's will and our mouth that speaks, continuously helping to create the world by our words. One figure who represents this energy is King David, who as God's anointed leader of the Jewish people established the first messianic kingdom in the land of Israel.[14] David received Divine energy, as *Malkhut* receives from all the levels above in the tree of the *sefirot*. Once, while traveling on the road, David was accosted by an enemy who cursed him aloud. David forbade his guard to kill the man, saying that because everything was from God, God also wanted him to hear the curses of this man.

David is also honored as the traditional writer of most of the Book of Psalms, which show him continually turning his heart to God and thereby turning himself into a receiver of energy. But he was not passive: He took the Divine energy he was given and transformed the Jewish world of his time by conquering Jerusalem and uniting the Israelite tribes into a strong nation.

Among women, *Malkhut* is represented by Esther, Queen of Persia, who is the heroine of the Purim story. She occupied a position of power, but used it in service of God and her people. On the surface, she appeared to be a passive recipient, merely one of the king's harem, taking instructions from Mordecai. But inwardly, she transformed herself into a powerful figure, who with wisdom, emotion, and passion, could turn the situation around and expose the wicked Haman. The words on the *Megillah,* the Purim scroll written by Esther, represent the transformative power of *Malkhut* in verbal form. Like Esther, we can receive from all the soul-qualities of thought, emotion, and action and use those forces, each in our unique way, to transform our world.

Fulfilling the Soul's Purpose

Now we can begin to see our task. An awesomely complex, transcendent entity enlivens our body and offers us its knowledge, sensitivity, and awareness. We want to be more and more open to this influence, to feel the soul and sense its messages. There are moments when we do have a sudden insight, and feel tingling up the spine or "goose bumps" in our flesh. There are times when, in an emergency, we completely lose our sense of self and know exactly what to do to save a life. Other times, we experience *deja vu,* telepathy or clairvoyance.

But most of the time, the work of the soul is hidden from us. Our main task is to clear the way for the soul to manifest itself, which means moving ego aside in daily life.[15] Too often, we seek pleasure and comfort, security and a sense of power or control over our lives. Sometimes these desires push God and spirituality totally out of the picture.

A sage of the Talmud once decided that these desires were too much for human beings to overcome. God would have to save us from ourselves. So the sage prayed with all his power for the "evil inclination," the *yetzer hara,* to be removed from the world. Because he was such a devout and saintly person, God granted his request.

The sage woke the next morning, expecting to see nothing but happiness and bliss. Sure enough, people seemed happy. But then it was discovered that chickens were not laying eggs, and ewes were walking away from their bleating lambs, since they were no longer interested in nursing them. Suddenly the sages realized that the *yetzer hara,* though often destructive, was also the passion that kept the world going. The issue is not to eliminate it, but to turn its energy to good use.

All our survival skills and ego defenses, all the emotions and passions that help us live in the world will eventually be turned to the good. All the scientific knowledge that shows us a natural world governed by regular laws will also reveal God. The distortion of ordinary reality, in which things do not appear to be part of God, will be clarified. How? Our own spiritual work provides the pivotal energy to reveal the concealed, by transforming our bodies, emotions, and minds into vessels of Godliness. By aligning ourselves—including our physical bodies—with our divine souls, we will complete the work of creation.

This is the purpose of Jewish life. The soul comes to live in the body to fulfill the Divine Will, which can only be fulfilled by the body and its organs. Fulfilling the "613 commandments" of the Torah—248 positive and 365 negative—purifies the body so that it can truly reflect the soul.[16] At the same time, the commandments enable the soul to purify its surroundings, because many commandments use physical objects—the yarn in the knotted fringes of a *tallit,* known as *tzitzit,* the greens atop the *sukkah,* the wax in Shabbat candles. The soul also encourages us to create a positive physical and emotional environment for spiritual development, to open up our houses, our rooms, and ourselves to others, rather than being overly self-concerned.

This is not about being perfect or making everything perfect. The soul knows that while everything ultimately comes from God, our world conceals the Divine. It is sensitive to what the body and mind do, and appreciates the difficulty of surviving in this world. The soul is the compassionate force in life. It knows the discipline that the body needs, and it encourages this with gentleness.

But the soul is also enriched by what it learns from the physical body. By learning about the profound difficulty of being human, it gains a respect for humanity. When the soul leaves this life, it will have learned things it could not learn in the highest world of souls. It will know not only that God is in what is good and great, but also that God is in the very worst and the very small.

To help you understand yourself as part of the greatness of God, here is a special meditation. We suggest that you incorporate colors into your visualization here. The ones we use are adapted from Jewish mystical traditions that correlate colors to the *sefirot.* In Kabbalah as in some other mystical systems, colors tend to go from white or metallic at the top of the body to red or purple at the bottom. But the system is somewhat variable. We encourage you to follow the color scheme that is most relaxing and comfortable to you.[17]

To help you locate God in the small things in your life, the meditation is followed by the Journal of the *Sefirot.*

Temple of the Soul

Visualize yourself walking toward a city in the early morning hours. Everything is quiet and fresh. You see in the distance, in a central plaza, a beautiful building of ancient stone, with arches and domes. It glistens in the light of the rising sun. It seems to be a temple of some kind.

As you approach, a robed figure greets you with a loving smile. You feel a sense of calm and intense happiness from this person. You are invited to come into the temple. As you enter, you see stained glass windows all around, in the domed ceiling, the arches, and the walls. Bright rainbows of light coming through them dance around the room. This seems to be a place of intense happiness and contentment.

In a central foyer, a chair is waiting for you. You sit down, facing the entrance. You realize this place was made for you. The whole of creation has been waiting for you to arrive here, and you realize that you now feel immensely happy.

You become aware that the light from the windows shines in a special way on you, as you sit in this chair. From the skylight at the top of the dome, a gentle white light streams down, caressing the top of your head and spreading gently over the surface of your body.

From the uppermost windows, a golden light enters, and the rays touch your right and left temple. They merge with the white light from above, and warm your face and neck.

Blue light streams in from the windows above and slightly to the front of you. Shades of blue illuminate your right and left shoulder. From the doorway, a clear sea-green light shines on your heart.

Light in reddish-orange tones comes from the windows behind you. The light warms your right and left hips, and spreads down your thighs. The light shines from behind on your lower back, and circles around your pelvis, warming your whole lower torso.

Now the marble floor itself begins to glow, warming your feet in its reflected light. Soon the lights on your body sparkle, making your whole body feel the dance of the lights, from top to bottom and side to side. Your body glows with energy.

Become aware of your breathing. As you breathe in, allow your body to expand. With each breath, allow the space your body occupies to expand a little more, while the lights in your body merge with the lights coming from the windows of the temple. As you expand, your space merges with that of the temple.

With each breath, allow yourself to expand still more. Your body is now entirely made of light, and you expand beyond the temple borders, beyond the city. Imagine yourself expanding still more, as much as you feel comfortable. You can expand out into space if you want.

When you have expanded as much as you like, rest and breathe deeply. Be aware how your light is connected to all the other light in the universe. Rest, and feel the happiness of being connected to everything, and to the Source of everything.

When you are ready, become conscious of your breathing again. With each exhalation, let yourself come back slowly, breath by breath, to the earth, to the city, to the temple. Breath by breath, come back to your chair, where you are glowing with light and energy.

When you are ready, rise from the chair and depart, knowing that you can return here anytime. And you are taking with you the glow of the lights, and the glow of the happiness you felt here.

Journal of the *Sefirot*

It is important to find some time to reflect on the work we do on ourselves—our prayers in the morning, our meditations, and our interactions with the world throughout the day. The tradition of the Jewish bedtime prayers (the bedtime *Shema* and accompanying prayers and blessings) encourages us to take a few minutes to think about our day before going to sleep. For this purpose, we have designed the Journal of the *Sefirot*.

You can photocopy the pages that follow, or use them as an outline for your own notebook. Keep it by your bed to remind you to review your day before going to sleep. The questions are suggestions for ways of thinking about the different areas of your life. It is not necessary to answer all the questions every day; and some evenings you may just want to read over the questions. We do encourage you to spend ten or fifteen minutes mentally reviewing your day, and to make at least one notation each day. On Friday afternoon before Shabbat, you may want to review the notes you've made during the week.

Most of us have difficulty staying with such a discipline consistently.

Don't judge yourself if you forget, or if you don't want to do it for awhile. The Journal is something you can return to as a grounding for spiritual growth. Even if you don't use it regularly, you can turn to it at difficult times in your life, or use it as Rosh Hashanah and Yom Kippur approach. See the Journal of the *Sefirot* as a tool for your own self-understanding.

Chochmah (Wisdom): How did God place wisdom in my path today? Was my mind clear enough to receive it? For example, when I listened to another person, was there something special in their words for me? Or did I open a book and find something I needed for my growth?

Take a moment to ask God to show you wisdom and direct you in each moment.

Binah (Understanding): How did God help me integrate new information today? Where were my thoughts? Was my mind critical or judgmental? Did I exercise it with something challenging? Was my mind connected to important things or obsessing over trivialities?

Ask God for the ability to see the connections in everything that happens, everything you learn, and to use the information that comes to you for good.

Daat (Knowledge): How did God help me connect mind and heart today? Did I pray? Did I express myself in a heartfelt way to someone else? Am I holding back on things I need to express? Are there words stuck in my throat? Can I write them down instead? Or am I wasting words in idle chatter?

You can ask God to help you speak from the heart, in prayer and in conversation, and direct your words where they will do the most good.

Chesed (Lovingkindness): How did I experience my own acts of loving today? Am I balanced in my expression of love? Am I trying to give too much? Am I manipulating or suffocating others with my kindness? Or am I withholding my love to serve myself? Did I offer kindness to someone else—a smile, an offer of help, hospitality?

Pray that God will help you find the right expression of love, to bring light to others, and enable others to grow from your loving them.

Gevurah (Strength): How did God help me restrain myself emotionally? Did I protect myself from giving too much, or from seeking others' approval? What boundaries do I need in order to maintain my sense of self? Did I discipline my time to allow for prayer and self-reflection? What other discipline or rules did I observe today?

Ask God to show you how to develop inner strength and self-restraint.

Tiferet (Harmony): Did God warm my heart today? Was there anything that brought tears to my eyes, or allowed me to open up and breathe more freely? Was my heart filled with truth? Did I have a sense of integrity? Did I harden my heart in fear or anger? Can I forgive myself and others for what did not seem to go right?

Pray for forgiveness, and the ability to forgive. Ask God to soften the hardness of your heart and let it fill with warmth.

Netzach (Perseverance): How did God help me move forward today? Where am I being led in my connection to God's will? Was I overworking or pushing too hard? Or was I holding back, not putting my energy wholeheartedly behind what I was doing? Where did I lose patience?

Ask God for patience and endurance, and pray for the ability to connect to God's will at every new step.

Hod (Balance): How did God offer me support today? What people and activities in my life gave me confidence, appreciation and encouragement? What doors are opening for me that I have not been paying enough attention to? What am I complaining about, and how can I change or accept it? Is my own will in the way?

Ask for guidance on how to see your life as a connected, flowing whole. Pray for any support you may need at this moment.

Yesod (Creative Energy): How was God directing me toward my own creative energy today? Was I in touch with my dreams and passions? Was I pursuing goals of money, power, and prestige? Or was I using my creative energy in tune with my divine spirit? How did I use my sexual energy? Was I greedy? Was I aware when I had enough? Did I set aside money or time for some charitable purpose?

Ask God to heighten your awareness of how you use your creative power, and to direct it into Godly channels.

Malkhut (Manifestation): Were my actions today directly connected to God's will, or was I following my personal will based on my ego? Were my actions for my *highest* good? Was I conscious of acting with a view toward my spiritual destiny, or only toward material and immediate needs? Did my actions consider other people? Did I act with consideration of future consequences? If I had to leave this life tomorrow, would I be satisfied with what I did today?

Take one more moment to ask God to teach you how you can make a difference even in small things; how you can connect to the grand design in your everyday acts; what you are meant to do here, as a soul manifesting its presence on earth.

Elohai Neshamah: Movement and Meditation

Let us return now to the morning blessings with special meditations for the soul.

First say the prayer, then do the exercise and close with a short meditation.

אֱלֹהַי, נְשָׁמָה שֶׁנָּתַתָּ בִּי טְהוֹרָה הִיא. אַתָּה בְרָאתָהּ,
אַתָּה יְצַרְתָּהּ, אַתָּה נְפַחְתָּהּ בִּי, וְאַתָּה מְשַׁמְּרָהּ בְּקִרְבִּי.
וְאַתָּה עָתִיד לִטְּלָהּ מִמֶּנִּי, וּלְהַחֲזִירָהּ בִּי לֶעָתִיד לָבֹא.
כָּל־זְמַן שֶׁהַנְּשָׁמָה בְקִרְבִּי, מוֹדֶה אֲנִי לְפָנֶיךָ, יהוה אֱלֹהַי
וֵאלֹהֵי אֲבוֹתַי, רִבּוֹן כָּל־הַמַּעֲשִׂים, אֲדוֹן כָּל־הַנְּשָׁמוֹת.
בָּרוּךְ אַתָּה, יהוה, הַמַּחֲזִיר נְשָׁמוֹת לִפְגָרִים מֵתִים.

El-o-hai, ne-sha-ma she-na-ta-ta bi, t'ho-rah hi. A-ta v'ra-tah, a-ta ye-tzar-ta, a-ta n'fach-ta bi. V'a-ta m'sham-ra b'kir-bi, v'a-ta a-tid lit-la mi-mei-ni, u-l'ha-cha-zi-rah bi le-a-tid la-vo. Kal z'man she-ha-n'sha-ma v'kir-bi, mo-deh a-ni l'fa-ne-cha, A-do-nai el-o-hai v'el-o-hei a-vo-tai, Ri-bon kal ha-ma-a-sim, A-don kal ha-ne-sha-mot. Ba-ruch a-ta A-do-nai, ha-ma-cha-zir ne-sha-mot lif-ga-rim me-tim.

My God, the soul that You have placed in me is pure! You created it, You formed it, You breathed it into me. You safeguard it within me, and eventually You will take it from me and restore it to me in time to come. As long as the soul is within me, I gratefully thank You, Adonai, my God and the God of my ancestors, Master of all works, Lord of all souls. Blessed are You, Adonai, who restores souls to dead bodies.

"...the soul which You have placed in me is pure!"

1. Close your eyes and imagine a pure spark from God floating down from above toward you. Raise your hand and receive the spark in your fingertips with a sense of awe.

"You created it, You formed it..."

2. Bring the spark near to your heart, then release it from your fingertips. Your fingers and hand open like a flower blooming.

3. Form an imaginary ball of pure soul energy in front of your chest, rotating your hands as if sculpting clay.

"...You breathed it into me."

4. Bring the soul energy toward your face and mouth, allowing it to spray your face as with a fresh mist. Take it in with a deep, audible inhale through your mouth. Let your arms drop down to the sides of your body.

"You safeguard it within me..."

5. Embrace yourself, body and soul with your arms: The left arm wraps around the right side of your body, and the right arm wraps across the front of the body.

"I gratefully thank You... Master of all works, Lord of all souls."

5. With arms still wrapped, bow to the east, west, north, and south (or front, back, side, side). Circle the whole upper body, from the waist up, to the right, then to the left.

"Blessed are You...who restores souls to dead bodies."

6. Now imagine your body becoming the image of a soul: Think of a cool, pastel rainbow as a flame of energy inside your body. Allow a gentle swaying motion to start at the soles of your feet, and let the swaying come all the way up your body. Raise your arms and continue the swaying upward so that the arms become the tip of the flame. Let your whole body become the radiant flame of the soul.

Meditation

Close your eyes. Breathe deeply. Visualize two Shabbat candles being lit. The match of inspiration touches the wick and a flame ignites. The light spreads all around you, lighting the whole room. The radiant flame reaches upward toward its Creator and the world from which it came. The flame knows that it is here to light the world, and that when it is done, it will return to its Creator knowing it has fulfilled its purpose. Imagine yourself as this pure light, reaching toward God and shining out with knowledge and action to fulfill our work on earth. As you go through your day, remember your light, and see around you the lights of the others you encounter, all part of the One.

אֵלּוּ דְבָרִים שֶׁאֵין לָהֶם שִׁעוּר: הַפֵּאָה, וְהַבִּכּוּרִים,
וְהָרֵאָיוֹן, וּגְמִילוּת חֲסָדִים, וְתַלְמוּד תּוֹרָה.

אֵלּוּ דְבָרִים שֶׁאָדָם אוֹכֵל פֵּרוֹתֵיהֶם בָּעוֹלָם הַזֶּה וְהַקֶּרֶן
קַיֶּמֶת לוֹ לָעוֹלָם הַבָּא: וְאֵלּוּ הֵן: כִּבּוּד אָב וָאֵם, וּגְמִילוּת
חֲסָדִים, וְהַשְׁכָּמַת בֵּית הַמִּדְרָשׁ שַׁחֲרִית וְעַרְבִית. וְהַכְנָסַת
אוֹרְחִים וּבִקּוּר חוֹלִים וְהַכְנָסַת כַּלָּה וּלְוָיַת הַמֵּת וְעִיּוּן תְּפִלָּה
וַהֲבָאַת שָׁלוֹם בֵּין אָדָם לַחֲבֵרוֹ וְתַלְמוּד תּוֹרָה כְּנֶגֶד כֻּלָּם.

These are the things that have no prescribed measure: the corner of a field [that must be left for the poor], the first-fruit offering, pilgrimage [to Jerusalem], acts of kindness, and Torah study. (*Mishnah Peah* 1:1)

These are the things whose fruits a person enjoys in this world, and the principal remains for him in the World to Come. They are: honoring father and mother, acts of kindness, coming early to the house of study morning and evening, hospitality to guests, visiting the sick, providing for a bride, escorting the dead, absorption in prayer, bringing peace between one human being and another—and the study of Torah is equivalent to them all. (Talmud, *Shabbat 127a*)

6
Our Walk on Earth

Acting in the World

ONCE WE'VE ALIGNED body, mind, and soul, it is possible to take a new look at ourselves. We have made more room in our lives for personal prayer, and it's now possible to hear the still small voice of the soul. At least some of the time, we can look at things from a different and higher perspective, a more Godly perspective. With our knowledge of the *sefirot,* we can perceive ourselves in a higher form, in light of the anatomy of our souls.

But now it's natural to ask: Where do we go from here? Is there a new direction for us, a special orientation? Is there some further purpose?

Becoming more spiritual doesn't necessarily mean exhibiting great outward changes. One doesn't have to leave one's job and go to rabbinical school. Most important is a shift in perspective, in how we look at the world and define it, in our ultimate goals and values and our commitment to them. The changes we make are small but significant, like the morning prayers and exercises we have learned.

Our bodies are more than complex self-enclosed entities. We were given feet, hands, and mouths to extend ourselves outward, to bring our energy into the world. Among the *sefirot, Malkhut* is represented by the feet and also by the mouth with its power of communication outward. The way we move, the way we act and speak toward others are the results of all our spiritual work.

The "walking-way" in Judaism is called *halachah*. Its world, the world of action in Jewish tradition, is guided by the concept of *mitzvah*. The word is usually translated as "commandment," but its root, *tzv,* connotes "connection" or "binding." Essentially, it means an act that connects you, the world, and God.

This is a very simple concept, and it's important to hold onto its simplicity. The word *mitzvah* tells us: Make a connection. We don't have to think of *mitzvot* as a grand system in which you have to do everything, or do nothing. In any given moment, we can act in a way that *connects.* Sometimes we connect to God, sometimes to ourselves, sometimes to other people. In any moment, you can turn your face toward God's light, and experience *teshuvah,* a "return." In any moment, you can shine your own light toward someone else and help transform your life and theirs.

Crossing Over

How to do this? The above passages from the Oral Torah, which we recite after the morning blessings over the Torah, suggest that there is a particular Jewish way to act, a particular emphasis of the *mitzvot.* We can see this most clearly if we analyze them separately.

The first quotation, from the Mishnah (the primary written explanation of the Torah's laws), talks about *mitzvot* that have no specific measure, that you can do as much or as often as you want: leaving the corner of your field for the poor to gather, bringing first fruits of your crop to the Temple in Jerusalem, going on the three holiday pilgrimages, acts of kindness, and studying Torah. Technically, the first three are not applicable outside of Israel or when there is no Temple in Jerusalem, but the principle is clear and applicable wherever we are. Giving to others, offering of yourself to God, and improving yourself through Torah learning are powerful acts of healing. Their effects ripple outward indefinitely, and you can devote yourself to them as fully as you want. These are basic, fundamental ways of connecting to Godliness.

The second passage, from the Gemara (the Talmudic discussions of the Mishnah), also talks about quantity, but in a different way: We receive "interest" (fruits) on certain *mitzvot* in this world, but the "principal" isn't touched; it will be waiting for us in the next world. These Talmudic economics may seem a little strange, but the Sages are trying to tell us that, while we frequently cannot see the effects of our actions, certain acts do bring spiritual results in this world. When we get involved in such activities, our lives will be better, longer, and healthier. We will become more sensitive and our connections to other people will be enhanced. Further, these same actions have effects on our souls. In the World-to-Come, the world where our true souls will shine forth, these will be the things from which we learned the most, and which counted most in our long-term spiritual development.

What are these acts of great goodness? Here they are in list form:

☐ Honoring our parents

☐ Acts of kindness

☐ Attending the "house of study"—the synagogue—morning and evening

☐ Hospitality to guests

☐ Visiting the sick

☐ Rejoicing with a bride and groom

☐ Escorting the dead to the grave

☐ Being absorbed in prayer

☐ Bringing peace between people

☐ Studying Torah

What makes these *mitzvot* so special that their rewards would be in both this world and the next? If we look at them carefully, we see that many of these *mitzvot* get us involved with people who are in an unusual situation or who have a special status. Parents represent the previous generation, people who have a different life-perspective from our own. Guests are outsiders, usually temporary visitors. (Friends or next-door neighbors can also be guests, but the *mitzvah* of *providing* for a guest is obviously greater for someone who is truly in need.) The sick temporarily cannot contribute to life in their normal ways. A bride and groom are assuming a dramatically new status and often need financial or emotional support. Those who have died are clearly in a different state of being, having left this world and being in passage to a different one. And people in conflict with others are emotionally cut off from normal relationships.

These *mitzvot* are not simply a matter of providing for those in need, for only some of these people are "needy." But each of them does demand that we relate to those who are out-of-place in some way, such as being dis-located or in transition. When we relate to these different kinds of people with kindness, we make connections across boundaries. We move out of our egotistical worlds to offer ourselves to others. Taking on such obligations is not always easy. Attending funerals is often difficult, getting in the middle of someone else's fight is usually stressful, and visiting the sick can be an inconvenience. But in doing so, we open doorways, and we serve as examples for others to do the same. We become *Ivrim,* a Hebrew word for "Jews" that means, those who "cross over," those who are the connectors in the world.

From this perspective, the list comes more clearly into focus. When we are in a synagogue, ready to pray or learn, we make a profound connection to our tradition. We "cross over" and establish ourselves in God's world, a spiritual world. We also become door-openers for others, welcoming them into the place of study and prayer, helping them cross the boundary from the ordinary world into a more holy one. Being absorbed in prayer means that we are making an effort to connect deeply to the meaning of the words of prayer, and to have *kavannah* ("intention") as we pray, so that we can "cross over" to God. In studying Torah we struggle to learn a different point of view, to see things from God's perspective.

Other *mitzvot* do this as well. When we make Shabbat or celebrate a *Yom Tov* (holiday), we step out of ordinary time into a cyclical time that connects us with the rhythm of creation and with the Jewish community through the ages. Our ability to do this bolsters us when we act in the present world.

Gemilut chasadim, acts of kindness, is the remaining category on the Gemara's list. Something is odd about this category: It is general, while all the rest are quite specific. Yet even that teaches us something. Every time we do an act of kindness, every time we move beyond ourselves, we cross a boundary and relate to others wherever they are. When we use our mouths for kind words, when we speak gently and appreciatively, we erode the walls that gossip and criticism have built. This helps dissolve the *kelipot* or "husks" of evil that hide the good in the world.

Most of us know (though we often forget) that helping others can bring a special joy. When we do it knowing that we are "doing a *mitzvah*," that we are creating and strengthening bonds and connections, we can be even happier because then we know we are doing the will of God. As the Hasidic scholar, Rabbi Schneur Zalman of Liadi, wrote in his classic work of mysticism known as the *Tanya,* our bodies become extensions of God. The mouth that gives a warm greeting is God's mouth, the hand that gives aid to a poor family is God's hand, the feet that walk as we accompany a funeral procession are God's feet [1] When hundreds of arms make *challah,* when hundreds of heads wear *tefillin,* when hundreds of mouths speak Torah, we become a vast body resonating in harmony. Since we connect across time as well, interweaving with other generations, our Jewish body becomes timeless. In this perspective, even the smallest acts become powerful.

The Royal Way: A Parable

In these acts of crossing-over, we are not "merging" with God or with others. We are building bridges. We maintain our uniqueness—as Jews, as individuals, as human beings in physical form—while connecting with those who are different. We acknowledge that others may not be like us, and we are trying to bring them some of God's Light as it is refracted through the perspective of our unique soul.

This is why it is significant that as Jews, we are rooted in Jewish identity and tradition. Jews have a collective soul-contract, known as the *brit* or covenant, during their stay on earth, in addition to the individual purposes that each soul has. The covenant means that we are committed to be ambassadors of God on earth, exemplifying God's ways just as the officials of a consulate represents its nation's culture and laws even when inside the territory of another nation.

The commitment to this covenant, and trying to apply it to every situation, brought about the tradition of Jewish law which is, we might say, the Jewish spiritual path. The complex system of laws that make up *halachah* is the result of the effort, over three thousand years, to be thorough and consistent about our obligations to the covenant, to bring the Divine Light into our lives and the lives of others. Specific laws might address the details of Shabbat observance or business ethics, the use of advanced medical technology or the joy of dwelling in a *sukkah,* but each law is connected to the greater purpose of affirming God's presence everywhere and in everything. Ultimately, what Jewish law tries to do is coordinate the thousands of legs that are trying to walk along God's path and create a powerful dance.

Sometimes, to modern American Jews, this way of walking doesn't seem to fit, although at some level we realize that being Jewish gives us a special heritage and a unique perspective on life. In fact, we may criticize our synagogues for not being spiritual enough, or our charitable organizations for being too bureaucratic, or ourselves for not doing enough to live a Jewish life. The struggle to integrate our own personal development with a community standard and with God's will for us is common, and every person negotiates it differently. Sometimes, following one *halachah*—one walking-step—is our task for the day. Since we can't walk in one another's shoes, we cannot dictate to each other what steps to take.

The important point is to remember that God wants us to make the connections and shine the Light. Too often we assume that God is an angry, punishing figure, but this is really only a manifestation of our own most judgmental selves.[2] God is, after all, our Creator and a most loving parent. Such a parent loves the child unconditionally. When loving parents watch their child play, every little thing the child does delights them. Every time the child attempts something new or accomplishes a task, the parents are pleased. God looks at us much the same way: Every time we do something positive, God is delighted. But even more than an earthly parent, God knows how difficult it is to act rightly in this world. When we act like human beings—like a *mensch,* the Yiddish expression for a responsible person—God is very happy. Every *mitzvah* is one of those acts of *menschlichkeit,* of deep humanity.

At the same time, children thrive when they have clear boundaries, and sometimes even need punishment as a correction for deceit or disobedience. Unfortunately, many modern Jews see God's discipline only from a child's perspective, as the angry parent, and they miss the God who is unconditional love. We read biblical stories of God's anger or disappointment and are startled that God decreed death for disobedience. We forget that death is not the ultimate punishment—separation from God is.

Most of the time God, like the loving parent, just wants us to keep growing—spiritually. Of course, if children experience difficulty or disability, the parents will still love them, but they grieve over the problem until it is solved. Likewise God grieves when we allow our lives to stagnate, but still loves us and keeps sending us messages and offers of help. We can respond by being thankful when things go smoothly, instead of taking them for granted. When someone says just the right word that touches our hearts or brings tears to our eyes, we can hear it as God's word to us. We can be open to what God is doing by being present in the moment. Ultimately, God wants us to find our own unique spiritual, emotional, and physical expression of Godliness, through returning to a relationship with our Divine Source.

Sometimes, we give up on ourselves and on God, and we forget to aspire to Godliness. A Hasidic story offers a parable for our situation:

Once a king sent his son away to make his own living, in order to build his character. He kept track of the son by sending his servants as spies. They watched that the young prince did not get into great danger, and reported back on how he was doing. The prince was not very fortunate in his endeavors, however, and he ended up barely eking out a living as a peasant working the land of a wealthy nobleman.

Now the king had the custom of visiting his provinces from time to time to offer his subjects the chance to make requests of him. During those special visits, a person could go to the king personally and ask for anything he wanted. Eventually, he came to the province where his son was. The prince's friends encouraged him to come along to the audience with the king, and ask for relief from his difficulties.

When everyone lined up to see the king, the monarch saw his son in the line. He could hardly wait to speak to him, for he really missed his son and wanted him back. Finally, the son's turn came, and he humbly presented his request. "Could I have some warm clothes to get me through the winter?"

The king's face fell. "This is what you want?" he said, "A new set of clothes?"

"Yes, please," said the king's son.

The king looked up sadly. "I can give you clothes," he said. "But you could have had anything you asked. Why didn't you ask to be brought back to my palace and reinstated as prince of the land?"

This story tells us, first, that just as the king believed his son could pass all the tests, God—*Avinu Malkenu,* Our Father, Our King—has complete confidence that we can live to a high standard. We can be God's ambassadors on earth. Any obstacles we encounter on the way to this goal are tests or means of refinement. Even more, just as the king loved his son and was eager for his return, God is ready to help us in any way. In fact, God is waiting for us to ask, so that God can shower us with blessings. Third, we are setting our sights too low. We don't believe that we are really daughters and sons of the King, and that we belong in the palace.

Perhaps the prince had become depressed because of his exile, and the more he was away, the more he thought he couldn't fulfill all the obligations of his station. While living in the palace, he had a good tutor, and those around him set fine examples and offered him good advice. But after years as a poor peasant, he felt himself unequipped to live with royalty.

All of us often feel unequipped, but this is because of our "exile," both the general human condition and the specific exile of the Jewish people from their land. The Torah puts forward an ideal path of action—of Godly behavior—but we often haven't had the "tutors" to help us understand it or the "advisers" to set examples for us to emulate. But, the story tells us, this doesn't matter. We can still return to the palace as princes and princesses. God is ready to help us, to set the forces of the universe in motion on our behalf, if we will just turn our faces to the Light, orient ourselves toward God.

Being of royal lineage means that we have a sense of obligation for the world. As princely ambassadors, we are responsible for the direction the world takes, and for modeling to others the best kinds of behavior. God has confidence that all of us, together and individually, can meet that obligation. We can "cross over," connect to God, and reach out to others in a spirit of giving. We can play a major role in bringing the Divine Presence into the world.

Gift Meditation

You are sitting on ancient stone boulders in front of a lake that is clear as glass. Beauty surrounds you. The tall trees that are mirrored in the water frame the lake. The sky is a crystal blue and the air smells fresh. The sun gently bathes you with its warm golden light. The breeze caresses you like loving hands.

Breathe in and exhale deeply. Rest, and feel how perfectly the rocks cradle you.

As you relax, feel your body begin to drain of its tense, nervous energy. The stones behind you are unique, for they are able to absorb negative energy and make it disappear. You will feel a gentle pull or drawing out in each area of your body that needs to release negative energy. You will experience a cleansing.

As you lie still, breathing in and out, you feel a gentle pull in the back of your head. Feel your mind release and relax. Any chatter, confusion, or mental blocks drain into the rocks, leaving your mind clear and clean.

Feel a pull in the back of your neck, as your throat center empties and frees itself of negative words, words that have hurt or caused fear. The obstacles that accumulate in the throat and choke your self-expression move outward and disappear. Your throat is clear, and you know you can speak freely from your heart.

A gentle pull arises between your shoulder blades as your heart region empties of pain, hurt, and sadness. Your heart feels clean and begins to open like a flower. The drawing energy pulls a little below the heart, underneath the shoulder blades. The area where you hold your emotions relaxes, and discomfort or pressure in that area releases into the rocks beneath you.

There is a tug at the lower back as your belly drains of tension and pain. Your hips slowly release their energy into the base of your spine, and they also are free of tension. Your legs relax, allowing fatigue to leave through the back of your thighs and the soles of your feet. Tension in your arms drains out through the palms of your hands.

Become aware of a clean inner self—emptiness, purity, and freedom. Enjoy the feeling of being an open vessel, ready to receive.

Look in front of you at the clear glass lake. In its mirror, see yourself as a joyful being, your face filled with light. Take the time to enjoy yourself in this way.

Now allow an image to appear in front of you, an image of something you do that makes you whole and joyful. Allow it to revolve in front of you very slowly, like a Ferris wheel. Let another picture appear, and add it to the wheel.

Add more pictures as they arise of happy, wholesome parts of your life. Let your mind think of people who love you, the exercises you do to take care of your body, the healthy foods you eat, the prayers you say, the activities that give you a positive sense of accomplishment, the people you have helped, the ways you improve your mind, the ways you develop your talents. If there are things you don't now do but would like to add, allow them to join the revolving wheel.

Now encircle this vision with white light. Begin to breathe in the light. You will breathe in three times, bringing the vision into your heart along with the light.

First, breathe in and hold your breath.

Exhale any doubts or fears that may be in your way.

Again, breathe in and hold, allowing the feeling of the vision to be sweet and rich in your chest. Exhale any obstacles that are still there.

Once more: Breathe in deeply, hold your breath, and let the vision take hold. Exhale any remnants that are in its way. Release any tension in your chest and arms.

You may feel a tingling in your body. This is the body's new potential, joining its energy with your inner self. Feel it also integrating into the mind and soul. Your body-mind-and-soul are creating and experiencing wholeness. Keep breathing. Delight in the grace you have been given.

Shekhinah: The Presence

This is what the tenth *sefirah, Malkhut,* is about: "Presence." On the individual level, *Malkhut* is the totality of the person, the wholeness of the self that has received from all the other *sefirot.* Every impression you have received from outside, every thought and image that your mind has processed, all the feelings you have felt, all the movements you have made, pour into *Malkhut.* Your presence when you walk into a room is the embodied expression of this *sefirah*—the unique way you walk, the way your hands gesture in the air, the tone of voice that is distinctively yours.[3]

Because *Malkhut* is the result of what we have "received" from God, we tend to think that it is genetic or comes from early conditioning. We've heard such statements as "Your voice sounds just like your mother's," or "You walk just like your father." To be sure, our parents give us a piece of their unique way of walking. But this is only the vaguest physical outline. Because we are embodied *souls*, we can also put a *spiritual* imprint upon our walk, our voice, our presence. As we sensitize each part of our body to the impression of the soul, as we use our minds to imagine and our hearts to feel spirit, our bodies begin vibrating to the tune of our souls.

As we perform those acts of building bridges to others and to God, we deepen and clarify that impression. The vibrations begin rippling outward, and our souls can be heard in our voice, felt in our presence, conveyed by the "impression" we make on others. This creates the symphony of the world, the dance of all its parts.

We each have our own ways of making these impressions and connections. Even our imperfections contribute, for every lesson that we've had to learn helps us integrate body and soul in a way that is unique. In each of us, our experience and learning flow into and through our minds and bodies, contributing to the kind of person we were meant to be.

That is how the Divine Presence, the *Shekhinah,* manifests itself. To the extent that every person manifests his or her soul through an embodied presence and through specific actions, the *Shekhinah* radiates more and more strongly. Every time human beings are present to one another, each trying to live in the light of God's teaching, each extending love, appreciation, and encouragement toward the other, each manifesting his or her unique qualities, the Divine Presence shines.

Admittedly, we can't always be wholeheartedly present in our actions. Sometimes we're withdrawn, angry, tired; sometimes we walk as if we're slogging through mud. But even if we take a half-step a little differently from the way we did the day before, we are making progress. As Psalm 34 says, "Turn away from evil and do good." If at least we can turn away from evil, we are putting ourselves in position to do good. If we can avoid answering someone with a sharp retort or not say something bad about others, if we can refrain from something that hurts ourselves or another person, these acts allow illumination to enter from the Divine Light.

Most of all, we can have faith that the vibrations of the universe are striving to be in harmony with one another, that the Divine Presence is striving to manifest itself, and it surrounds us all the time. We can help ourselves remember this by using one of the images for the *Shekhinah,* known as the Clouds of Glory. When the Jewish people came out from the slavery of Egypt, they traveled under a special protection and light, described in the Torah as "the pillar of cloud by day, and the pillar of fire at night" (Exodus 13:22, 40:38; Numbers 9:16-23). This was a special gift from God for the period of the desert travels: "When the cloud was raised up from the *Mishkan,* the Children of Israel would embark on their journeys" (Exodus 40:36; cf. Numbers 9:16-23). The *midrash* tells us that, as the well of water was given because of Miriam's goodness, and the manna because of Moses, so the cloud of protection was given because of the special qualities of their brother Aaron, the High Priest.

When God spoke to Moses, the Divine appeared as a cloud over the Tent of Meeting (Exodus 33:9, cf.34:5). On Sinai, the mountain was covered with a Cloud of Glory (19:16, 24:15-16), and the people "saw the voices" (20:15). Miraculously, the Presence could make itself felt in vibrations of sound that Moses's ear could hear and that the eye could sometimes see! Such encounters suggest that it was possible to have a physical sense of Presence, just as we can sometimes, on a much smaller scale, sense our own souls.

The *midrash* tells us that the Cloud that led the Jewish people in their travels actually manifested as seven clouds—one for each of the six directions (north, east, west, south, up, down), and a seventh that traveled in front of them and smoothed the trail. The people were entirely surrounded by the Divine Presence, and by its vibrations that offered them protection and light.

We invoke the Divine Presence when we say the *Mah Tovu,* creating "Sara's tent" which was also covered with a Divine Cloud; the traditional bedtime prayers also call forth the presence of angels in all directions, like the seven clouds.

But the Clouds teach us that even when we cannot sense the larger Presence, we still know that it is there. Every act we have done that has taken us out of our egos has helped to disclose the Presence.

So the Clouds also represent *emunah,* faith. We can walk the narrow bridge, and not fear. We can trust that the Cloud smoothes our way, that God is making all the bumps as small as possible for our growth and development.

When we are walking with faith, we make a statement to the world that there is a loving God who wants to be seen and felt in our lives. As we manifest our soul-energy more and more, as we put mind, body, and soul behind every action, the Presence will become more and more visible. The *Shekhinah* will show herself to be alive and well.

For Further Work

THE FOLLOWING MEDITATIONS can be used at different times for different purposes, depending on where you are in your "walk on earth." The first, the Walking Meditation, is recommended as a closing exercise for the morning blessings, but it can also be used at any time of the day. The second meditation, Angelic Clouds, which is adapted from a Jewish bedtime prayer, is calming and reassuring, for it reminds us of Divine protection and guidance. The colors used coordinate with traditional associations to some of the *sefirot*. As with all the meditations, relax and encourage yourself toward positive images and thoughts.

Walking Meditation

Our suggestion to people who want to get into better physical shape is to start like a baby: Learn how to walk. Map out the area where you plan to go. Twenty-five minutes is a good goal, but you might want to start with a five-minute walk. The main thing is to be consistent: three times a week, increasing ideally to five or seven times.

Use this time for prayer and personal time with yourself and with God. The rhythm of the walk and your own breathing are ways to align yourself with the rhythm of the loving God-mother who rocks you in Her arms, whose breath guides you on your way.

You can do this walk before or after you pray. Use it to release anxiety and become comfortable with your physical body. The healing power of a walk can be enhanced if you consciously allow God to walk with you.

Here are the steps:

1. *Walk in silence. For the first five minutes, be only your eyes. Take in every visual gift God is giving you—color, shape, shadow, movement.*
2. *For the second five minutes, be only your ears. Hear loud sounds, soft sounds, footsteps, silence, hear the* Shema.
3. *For the third five minutes, be only your sense of smell.*
4. *For the fourth five minutes, be your sense of taste. What does air taste like?*
5. *For the last five minutes, be your sense of touch. Pick up a rock or a leaf, and try to sense its vibration. Be aware of the soles of your feet and what they feel as they touch the ground with each step.*

When you return from the walk, you are ready to pray, meditate, or continue with your day. Our wish for you is that on every level you will feel more alive.

Angelic Clouds Meditation

This can be used at nighttime, just before bed, or anytime you need a calming meditation.

Sit in a relaxed position in a comfortable chair. You become aware of soft lights around you. As you look around, you see that each light comes from a cloud, and each has its own color.

On your right is a silver cloud, bringing you messages with all the information you need to move through your day. This represents the angel Michael, God's messenger.

On your left is a red cloud, filling you with strength and courage. This represents Gavriel, the angel of might.

In front of you is a bright golden cloud, shining a light on the path ahead of you. This represents Uriel, the angel of light.

Behind you is a soft, mint-green cloud, gently warming your shoulders. This represents Rafael, the angel of healing, bringing relief from the tensions and pains you tend to carry with you.

From above a clear white light gleams, shining like the rays of the sun through a cloud. Below your feet, the floor radiates with a clear blue light.

You can now recall the colors, throughout your day, to remind yourself that the Divine Presence hovers over you on your path.

Notes

Introduction

1. Rabbi Abraham Isaac Kook, "Lights of Renascence," sect 33, in *Orot* (1920), translated by Bezalel Naor (Northvale, N.J.: Jason Aronson, 1993), p. 189.

2. On the attempt to perfect the body, see Kenneth Dalton, *The Perfectible Body* (New York: Continuum Books, 1995), in which he traces the attempt to mold the body from the ancient Greeks down to contemporary body-builders.

3. Paraphrased from Rabbi Menachem Mendel Schneerson's interpretation of the Baal Shem Tov's story in *Likutei Sichot: An Anthology of Talks,* Vol. 4 (Brooklyn, N.Y.: Kehot Publication Society, 1992), note 106, p. 48.

4. As the MeAm Loez commentary explains this verse, we are forbidden to put ourselves in danger, including doing anything that might weaken our body (such as eating improper foods) or that might lead to illness. See Rabbi Yitzchaok Behar Argueti, *The Torah Anthology: MeAm Lo'ez,* translated by Rabbi Aryeh Kaplan, edit-

ed by Alexander Tobias (New York: Maznaim, 1984), Vol. 16, p. 90. The Talmud also states that "on Shabbat we do not exercise." From this, we can infer that the sages believed benefits could be gained from exercise on the remaining six days. The great seventeenth-century scholar and mystic, Rabbi Moshe Chaim Luzzatto, wrote that caring for the body helps ensure that the mission of the soul can be accomplished. See his *The Way of God,* translated and annotated by Rabbi Aryeh Kaplan (New York: Feldheim, 1983), section 1, paragraph 4.

In the thirteenth century, the Rambam (whom Christian sources call Maimonides), a physician as well as a great expositor of Jewish law and philosophy, insisted that the health and fitness of the body was a proper and central concern of the observant Jew. In his writings, particularly *Hilchot Deot 3*, he offered many recommendations for preserving and enhancing health. More recently, Rabbi Yisroel Salanter, founder of the nineteenth century *Mussar* movement that emphasized ethics and self-improvement, taught that the *mitzvah* of caring for one's health is, in a certain sense, greater than all the other *mitzvot* because, if it is ignored, you cannot do the others. Other great sages, such as the Chafetz Chaim, also taught about exercise, healthy food, and general fitness. They recognized that, in our increasingly sedentary society, such practices were essential to health. For a discussion of these, see Rabbi Moshe Goldberger et al., *Singing Hashem's Praises: Lessons from the Organs of the Body* (Staten Island, N.Y.: n.p., 1987), pp. 59-60.

Yet, Judaism has wrestled with the relation between the physical and the spiritual, as has much of Western philosophy. While there is no question that, from the Jewish perspective, the physical world is a creation of God and therefore good, God's demand that we "be holy as I am Holy" has sometimes been interpreted as requiring separation from the physical world. Hasidic thought, which is rooted in the mystical tradition, attempts to resolve the apparent contradiction by explaining that every created thing has a spark of divinity, but those sparks are concealed. Our task is to illuminate the physical world so that it clearly reflects God. This line of approach allows us to see holiness as potentially present in all aspects of ourselves, including our bodies. Through right thought, speech, and action we can reveal the Godliness that has been temporarily concealed. For a classic description of the "concealment" and levels of revelation, see Rabbi Moshe Chaim Luzzatto, *The Knowing Heart* (New York: Feldheim, 1982), pp. 239-245.

5. Visualization and meditation: Many styles and techniques of meditation are available today. Essentially, meditation is focused attention. When attention is focused, it can be used in several ways. The most common of these are: (1) calming and relaxing oneself into an altered state of consciousness or a mild self-hypnosis; (2) self-observation in order to gain awareness of and insight into our inner processes; and (3) visualization or contemplation, which involves using imagination to create an inner experience. Most meditations start with the first process and then move on to the second or third. Our meditations employ the third approach, encouraging the mind to focus on and become receptive to positive images, thoughts, and

sensations conceived in the imagination. Together with body movements, meditation helps imprint spiritual concepts more firmly in our physical beings.

Meditation is not an end in itself, but potentially an aid to achieving mental and emotional balance. In particular, meditation is *not* a substitute for prayer, which is essentially *Amidah*, a "standing" before God, in surrender to a higher Power. In the right framework, meditation can improve one's level of *kavannah* (spiritual intent) in prayer, and can help us develop a higher level of awareness and greater ability to serve God.

Deane Juhan, a theoretician of body work, offers an elaborate description of the power of thought and particularly of images and feelings evoked through meditation in *Job's Body: A Handbook for Bodywork* (Barrytown, N.Y.: Station Hill Press, 1987):

Man, in a way that was not possible before the elaboration of the cerebral cortex, is both freed and limited *by what he imagines* he can do. He has at his disposal hundreds of thousands of possible patterns of movement...[and] the ability to arrange these reflexes into as many new series as he wants. Yet he is powerless to organize these bits of motion into any purposeful sequence without *first imagining clearly* that sequence. An individual's relative strength of will and sense of coordination are in fact nothing other than his relative ability to imagine clearly and in detail those acts he wishes to accomplish....(pp. 291-92)

All reflex responses come under the control of the thought forms of the cortex, and any new sequence which can be clearly imagined can be learned; but on the other hand, this advancement of encephalization is not reversible, so that for us none but the most primitive orderly and purposeful sequences are possible without first imagining them clearly. And even more crucial... whatever elements are operative in our imaginations and our feeling states will find themselves inevitably expressed in our motor behavior, either as specific actions, as aberrations of those actions, or as the underlying style of actions in general....

This kind of meditation evokes feeling-states which then produces effects on the visceral muscles and blood chemistry. It has been verified that heartbeat and respiration slow down, use of oxygen drops, but blood flow to muscles increases, thus reducing lactate level in blood which cause pain and anxiety. Electrical resistance in the skin increases, also an indicator of lower anxiety, and the level of alpha waves in the brain rises. (p. 294)

6. Rabbi Nachman of Breslov, *Likutey Moharan,* Vol. 3, translated by Moshe Mykoff and annotated by Chaim Kramer (New York: Breslov Research Institute, 1990), Lesson 22, p. 340. Rabbi Nachman was a great-grandson of the Baal Shem Tov and the spiritual leader of the Breslover Hasidim at the turn of the nineteenth century. His teachings were recorded by his chief disciple, Rabbi Nosson of Nemirov.

7. On the manifestation of Godliness in the physical, see Luzzatto, *Knowing Heart,* p. 103: "Little by little, through virtuous acts, the soul effects...refinement in the body in proportion to its increased power, until the body is fit to present itself together with the soul, to behold the pleasantness of the Lord, and to sojourn in His sanctuary for all eternity."

   This idea is developed at much greater length in writings of the Hasidic tradition. For a contemporary presentation, see Shmuel Boteach, *When the Wolf Lies Down with the Lamb* (Northvale, N.J.: Jason Aronson, 1993).

Chapter 1

1. Rabbi Solomon Ganzfried, *Code of Jewish Law: A Compilation of Jewish Laws and Customs,* translated by Hyman E. Goldin (New York: Hebrew Publishing Company, 1963), p. 3; cf. also p. 1: "the soul, which was committed to God faint and weary, was restored to him renewed and refreshed."

2. There are more examples of giving the "first" to God: All first-born sons of a Jewish mother were originally to have been designated as Temple priests. The Levites or priestly tribe were later chosen to maintain the Temple for the whole Jewish people, but still the Torah instructs us to "redeem" the first-born sons (that is, to buy them back with money) so they can be freed from their Temple obligations. When bread is baked, a bit of dough must be set apart as the people used to do for the priests. The "taking of *challah*," as it is called, reminds us that we are consecrating our food. We also give *tzedakah* as the "first fruits" of the money we earn, for we view it as a gift from God.

   This principle also applies to how we dedicate our time. Judaism regards time as very important. Indeed, the first *mitzvah* given to the Jewish people was to set up a calendar ("This month shall be the beginning of months for you...the first of the months of the year," Exodus 12:1). As Rabbi Menachem M. Schneerson taught, "Man's best and quietest time each day is immediately after rising, for then his mind is calm. That time he must offer up to God, as it is said, 'The first of *arisotechem* you shall offer *challah.*'" The word *arisah* is generally translated as "dough," so that the word here means "your dough." But *arisah* can also mean a cradle or bed, so the verse can also be interpreted: "The first of your [rising from] bed you shall separate off as an offering" (*Likutei Sichot* on Parshas Korach, pp. 135-37). We also remind ourselves of the "priestly" nature of our service in another morning ritual. After saying *Modeh Ani,* we wash our hands ritually, using a cup to pour water over each hand alternately three times, then rinse our mouths. This also reminds us that we are entering into the service of God.

   The idea of being "priests" dedicated to divine service is explained by Rabbi Moshe Chaim Luzzatto in terms of being partners with God "like a woman with her husband," or "like two friends who incline to each other in love" (*Knowing Heart,* pp. 279, 281). Our task is to join with God for the purpose of perfecting the whole of creation. This demands that we disengage ourselves from personal desires, unite our hearts with God's purposes as revealed in Torah, and perform the *mitzvot* we are given (ibid., 297-303).

Chapter 2

1. This is the version of *Mah Tovu* in the prayerbooks with a standard Ashkenazi or Sefardi rite. A shorter version appears in the Chabad-Lubavitch prayerbook, which follows the *Nusach Ari,* the prayer rite of the famous sixteenth-century Kabbalist, Isaac Luria. Small differences in the wordings of certain prayers occur from one historical tradition to the next. The usual custom is to find out the historical community of one's father and learn that version, including the traditional pronunciation. Sometimes, when father and mother are from different communities, daughters will learn the prayer rite of their mothers.

2. The term "midrash" subsumes many different kinds of materials that offer interpretations of the biblical text. The collections of midrash known to us today were brought together in written form in, roughly, the fourth through eighth centuries, though their original sources undoubtedly go much further back in Jewish history. Midrash ranges from reliable oral tradition, to homily, to grand elaborations that use a considerable degree of poetic license. Even when traditions conveyed through midrash might be reliable, the rabbinic tradition recognizes that their main point is not to tell accurate history, but to inspire the reader.

   One familiar example of midrash is the Passover *Haggadah,* which includes a section where biblical verses telling the Exodus are amplified, to dramatize *how* harsh the Egyptian slavery was, *how* numerous the people became, and so on. Midrash helps us to imagine not only the "facts" of the events, but their fuller implications and inner meanings. In the present case, when the midrash elaborates on Balaam's view of the Israelite tents, it tells us that the main point of his prophetic utterance was not to comment on the excellent physical construction of the tents, but on the spiritual values that the Israelite camp communicated through the positioning of the tents.

   The phrase "the midrash says," then, should be taken throughout not as an invocation of a historical source but as an introduction to a traditional spiritual interpretation, intended to enrich the images and thoughts available for our contemplation.

3. "Rashi" is an acronym for Rabbi Shlomo Yitzchak (anglicized as Solomon Isaac). Jewish scholars are frequently known by acronyms which have, over the centuries, become customary honorific names. Examples in this book are "the Ramban" for Rabbi Moshe ben Nachman, known in Christian sources as "Nachmanides"; "the Rambam" for Rabbi Moshe ben Maimon, also known as "Maimonides"; and "the Ramchal" for Rabbi Moshe Chaim Luzzatto. Alternatively, scholars may be known

by the title of one of their great works, as Israel Meir haCohen is known as the "Chafetz Chaim," after his book of the same title (which means "Who Desires Life"). While this may be confusing at first, when we accustom ourselves to these names, it becomes much easier to read discussions of the rich scholarly tradition that is our heritage.

4. Rabbi Matityahu Glazerson, *Torah, Light and Healing: Mystical Insights into Healing Based on the Hebrew Language* (Jerusalem: Lev Eliahu, 1993), p. 170, citing specifically the work of Rabbi Tzaddok HaKohen entitled *Pri Tzaddik*.

5. It is appropriate to imagine God's influx into the world in terms of "light," for this metaphor is elaborated at great length in Jewish mysticism. The mystics frequently use the term *Ein Sof* (the Infinite) for God in his Essence. When God began to create the world, God emanated a special Light. The mystics called this primal expression of Divinity the *Or Ein Sof,* Light of the Infinite.

    Light is such an apt metaphor for God's self-manifestation that, as Rabbi Avigdor Miller points out, it receives the longest blessing in our prayerbook. In the section of the morning service known as "the *Shema* and its blessings," the first blessing begins, "Blessed are You, Lord our God, Ruler of the Universe, who fashions light and creates darkness, who makes peace and creates all things." The blessing continues for several paragraphs before ending, "Blessed are You, Lord, who fashions the lights." The sages equate Divine light with the concepts of God's "holiness" and "glory." Moreover, because light made it possible to see, humans could learn from the universe to recognize the Creator: "The Light transformed Creation into a Torah which teaches." Therefore, Rabbi Miller advises, we should spend time meditating about light. See Avigdor Miller, *The Beginning: Comments and Notes on Breshis* (New York: Avigdor Miller, 1987), pp. 18, 20.

    Finally, the numerological value of the Hebrew word for lights, *orot,* is 613—the number of Divine commandments in the written Torah. See Glazerson, *Torah, Light and Healing,* p. 120.

6. On the menorah, see Glazerson, *Torah, Light and Healing,* pp. 55-56.

7. The quotation from the midrash can be found in Raphael Patai in *Man and Temple* (New York: Ktav, 1967), p. 114. The Talmud has many ways of understanding the parts of the body besides the analogy to the *Mishkan.* For an encyclopedic treatment, see Avraham Yaakov Frankel, *In My Flesh I See God: A Treasury of Rabbinic Insights About the Human Anatomy* (Northvale, N.J.: Jason Aronson, 1995).

Chapter 3

1. Rabbi Avigdor Miller, *A Kingdom of Cohanim: Commentary and Notes on Vayikra* (New York: Avigdor Miller, 1994), p. 35.

2. Rabbi Aryeh Kaplan explains the expression "the soul is in the blood," in his translator's note to Luzzatto's *The Way of God,* p. 347:

> The nerves, as well as the veins and arteries, are said to contain a type of "blood," but that in the nerves is its highest fraction. The only thing that flows through the nerves, however, is the neural impulses, and therefore these impulses must be considered the highest fraction of the "blood"....According to this, the "animal soul," which is the information in man's brain as well as his ability to process it, would depend on this "blood," namely the neurological processes. This is the meaning of the statement that the "soul is in the blood."

Avraham Greenbaum amplifies our understanding of the liquid circulation in the body in his discussion in *Wings of the Sun: Traditional Jewish Healing in Theory and Practice* (Jerusalem: Breslov Research Institute, 1995), p. 175:

> Even blood as we think of it is far from being a simple, uniform fluid. In its colorless plasma float millions of red cells, white cells and platelets. The red cells transport vital oxygen....The various different kinds of white cells play a vital role in defending the body against diseases, while the platelets cause the blood to clot. In addition, blood plasma is the vehicle for transporting the body's main fuels....Besides this, the blood transports hormones around the body; these are the chemical "messengers" that keep the various body parts and systems working harmoniously with each other, and influence our functioning in ways that medical science is only beginning to uncover.
>
> The red blood is thus crucial to the metabolism of all the cells of the body and to overall bodily functioning. If we then add the "life of the brain"—the neural impulses involved in sensory perception, physical movement, and the regulation of a wide variety of different bodily functions—when we talk about the "blood," we are talking about the key to the life of the entire body.

3. For an explanation of upper and lower waters based on Kabbalah, see Rabbi Yechiel Bar-Lev, *Song of the Soul: Introduction to Kaballa* (originally published in English under the title *Yedid Nefesh* [n.p., Israel: Petach Tikva, 1994] pp. 127-28).

4. This and most of the teachings about the breath and heart on the following pages are derived from Rabbi Nachman of Breslov. See especially *Likutei Moharan,* Vol. 2, Lessons 8 and 13, and Volume 3, Lesson 21.

5. Rabbi Nachman of Breslov, *Likutey Moharan,* Vol. 3, Lesson 19, pp. 157-59 and n. 95. On the number thirty-two: the thirty-two occurrences of God's name are called, in Kabbalah, the "thirty-two *Elohim* of the Act of Creation." The famous Kabbalist Isaac Luria understood these to allude to the twenty-two letters of the Alef-Bet plus the ten *sefirot.*

The systems of *gematria* can be complicated, but the most basic one is easy to learn. In it, the letters of the Hebrew alphabet are assigned numbers as follows:

alef	א	1	yud	י	10	koof	ק	100
bet	ב	2	kaf	כ	20	resh	ר	200
gimel	ג	3	lamed	ל	30	shin	ש	300
dalet	ד	4	mem	מ	40	tav	ת	400
heh	ה	5	nun	נ	50			
vav	ו	6	samech	ס	60			
zayin	ז	7	ayin	ע	70			
chet	ח	8	peh	פ	80			
tet	ט	9	tzadi	צ	90			

Thus the word for heart, *lev,* has the gematria of thirty-two (the numerical value of the word's letters: *lamed* = 30 and *bet* = 2). Also, as Rabbi Glazerson observes, the letters of *lev, lamed* and *bet,* are the last and first letters of the written Torah. They are the only two letters of the alphabet that can be combined with all four letters of God's holy name, *yud, heh,* and *vav,* to make meaningful words. He explains the meaning of this by saying, "The heart is the point through which one can become completely connected to his Creator." See Glazerson, *Torah, Light and Healing,* p. 29.

6. See Goldberger, *Singing Hashem's Praises,* p. 7.

7. Rabbi Nachman of Breslov, *Likutei Moharan,* Vol. 1, Lesson 3, pp. 33, 35.

8. Miller, *Kingdom of Cohanim,* p. 35.

9. For an excellent discussion of the "lost self" we seek in our potential partners, see Harville Hendrix, *Getting the Love You Want: A Guide for Couples* (New York: Harper Perennial, 1990). See also Nachum Braverman and Shimon Apisdorf, *The Death of Cupid* (Baltimore, Md.: Leviathan Press, 1996).

Chapter 4

1. Quotation is from Rabbi Nosson Scherman, commentary to *Siddur Kol Yaakov* (Brooklyn, N.Y.: Mesorah Publications, Artscroll Mesora Series, 1986), p. 16.
   On the *Torah Sheb'al Peh* (Oral Torah): Here is one helpful explanation of the function of the Oral Torah: Suppose you are committed to a moral principle—say, that animals should not suffer needlessly—and you want to act consistently with that principle. You will have to decide such things as: Can I wear leather belts and

shoes? Can I eat free-range animals who die of old age? If I do, do I have to consider that others might see me eating meat and get an appetite for meat themselves? Can I eat dairy foods, although the cow providing the milk from which it is derived may have suffered from not being allowed to live a normal life (feeding her calf rather than being milked by a machine)? Can I eat "natural" foods with such animal products as stearates and gelatin? Should I not eat meat even if refusing it hurts my grandmother's feelings? The multitude of decisions involved in trying to be committed to just one moral principle is mind-boggling. Judaism begins with ten basic principles—the Ten Commandments—and the Written Torah elaborates on them, resulting in the "613" *mitzvot* of the Torah. The Oral Torah contains the discussion of the various considerations involved in staying consistent—both in concrete practice (as defined in Jewish law) and in the spirit with which one lives life (the ideals and models expressed in our stories and parables, *aggada*).

2. Rabbi Abraham Isaac Kook, *The Lights of Penitence, the Moral Principles, Lights of Holiness, Essays, Letters, and Poems,* translated by Ben Zion Bokser (New York: Paulist Press, 1978), p. 110.

3. On *daat* and speech: Students of mysticism may recall that Kabbalah usually associates speech with the sefirah of *malkhut,* as part of our manifestation in the world. We are suggesting that there are two sorts of speech, one that is primarily *internal* verbalization, as in "talking to oneself," and one that is external, the attempt to communicate with others. It is possible to gain control over one's inner monologue, focus it as a soul-dialogue with God, and use it to change oneself. This is one of the purposes of prayer, as well as of affirmations and visualizations. While external speech is an expression of *malkhut,* internal speech is best understood as a work of *daat,* for it is focused on self-transformation. Rabbi Nachman also understands prayer as a means of increasing *daat,* along with observance of the three pilgrimage festivals (Pesach, Shavuot, and Sukkot). See Avraham Greenbaum, *Wings of the Sun,* especially chapter 18.

4. See Avraham Greenbaum, *Wings of the Sun,* for a recent treatment of Jewish approaches to healing. For recent research on the healing power of prayer, see Larry Dossey, *Healing Words: The Power of Prayer and the Practice of Medicine* (San Francisco: Harper Collins, 1993); Herbert Benson, *Beyond the Relaxation Response* (New York: Times Books, 1984), and Benson's *Timeless Healing* (New York: Scribner's, 1996).

5. See Rabbi Schneur Zalman of Liadi, *"Igeret HaTeshuvah,"* in *Likutei Amarim—Tanya* (Brooklyn, N.Y.: Kehot Publication Society, 1981), Chapter 10.

   The connection between mind and heart made by *daat* is a source of healing. This is signified by the *gematria* of the Hebrew words for brain and heart (*moach v' lev* = 86), which is the same as that of God's name *Elohim* The union of heart and brain connects human beings to the image of God within themselves. See Glazerson, *Torah, Light and Healing,* p. 63.

6. On the customs of prayer: The *siddur* or prayerbook gives the structure and content of prayers the year round, while for special prayers at certain times of the year—Rosh Hashanah, Yom Kippur, Sukkot—we have a *machzor* (meaning "cycle" of the year). There are some differences in the traditional texts or forms, according to customs of different Jewish communities. There are also traditional tunes. These traditions are known as *nusach.*

    Praying in one's own language is permitted if one understands no Hebrew, because one should understand what one is saying (*Sotah* 33a), but praying in Hebrew is preferred by all rabbinic authorities. As Rabbi Nosson Scherman, editor of the Artscroll siddur, explains, we have a responsibility to learn enough Hebrew to pray in *lashon kodesh,* "the holy tongue."

    The great Hasidic scholar, Rabbi Dov Ber, the Maggid of Mezritch, taught that Hebrew words have an inner connection with the created universe. If we look at the first verse of the Torah: *Bereishit bara Elohim et hashamayim v'et ha-aretz* ("In the beginning of the creation of heaven and earth..."), we find the word *et,* which is grammatically unnecessary. Made up of the letters *alef* and *tav,* the first and last letters of the Hebrew alphabet, it signifies that the letters were part of God's original creation. Moreover, as Rabbi Avigdor Miller points out, one of God's first acts was naming, calling the light *"yom"* and the darkness *"lailah."* For further explanation, see "Overview," *Siddur Kol Yaakov,* pp. xv-xvi; and Miller, *The Beginning,* p. 23.

    Normally, it is best to pray with a community because the group provides added spiritual strength for each individual's prayers, and because by doing so we affirm our oneness with the whole people. A *minyan* (quorum of ten) is required for certain prayers. But each individual is responsible to pray his/her own prayers, with their own tune, tempo, and voice level. Individuals pray in counterpoint, neither interfering with one another nor being expected to sing in unison. As the *siddur* says of the angelic beings who sing to God, "They give permission to one another" to praise God, each in its own way.

    The main function of the cantor is to lead the parts of the prayer where a *minyan* is required, for example: The *Kaddish* which ends each major section of prayer; the *Barchu,* which alerts the congregation to the beginning of the main portions (*Shema* and *Shemoneh Esreh* or *Amidah*); and the *Kedushah.* The *chazzan* also repeats the entire *Amidah* on behalf of anyone who could not or did not say it.

7. Rabbi Nachman of Breslov, *Likutey Moharan,* Vol. 1, translated by Simcha Bergman (New York: Breslov Research Institute, 1986), Lesson 2, p. 23.

8. Rabbi Nachman of Breslov, *Likutey Moharan,* Vol. 1, Lesson 5, p. 88.

9. *Your Word Is Fire: The Hasidic Masters on Contemplative Prayer,* edited by Arthur Green and Barry W. Woltz (Woodstock, Vt: Jewish Lights, 1993), pp. 49-50.

Chapter 5

1. The expressions "one-sixtieth of death...one-sixtieth of prophecy" have a specific significance in the context of Jewish scholarship. According to Jewish law, if a substance has less than one-sixtieth of some ingredient, that ingredient is "nullified"—it is of no legal significance in most cases. For example: If a small amount of milk falls into a pot of vegetable soup, such that the milk is less than one-sixtieth of the volume, the soup does not need to be considered dairy. On the other hand, if the milk constitutes one-sixtieth or more of the soup, the soup has enough of a "taste" of milk that it has become a dairy food.

   Thus, the expression "sleep is one-sixtieth of death" means that sleep is a "taste" of death. We can understand death and sleep by comparing them to each other, though death has many mysteries we cannot comprehend. Thus death, like sleep, is not a complete end to life. And sleep, like death, is a time when body and soul are separated—but not so completely as in death.

   With regard to dreams, Judaism regards them as mostly a processing of the day's experiences. But because "dreams are one-sixtieth of prophecy," dreams may also contain significant information, usually in coded form. Conversely, most prophets (Moses being an exception) received prophecy in dream-like states. For a treatment of traditional Jewish perspectives on dreams, with comments on how these relate to modern psychological interpretations, see Rabbi Shmuel Boteach, *Dreams* (Brooklyn, N.Y.: bp, 1991).

2. Rabbi Schneur Zalman of Liadi, *"Sefer Shel Benonim,"* in *Likutei Amarim—Tanya,* Chapter 19, pp. 77-79. The image comes from a quotation in Proverbs 20:27: "The spirit of man is the candle of God."

3. Rabbi Menachem M. Schneerson, *The Chassidic Dimension,* Vol. 1, compiled by Rabbi Sholom B. Wineberg and edited by Uri Kaploun (Brooklyn, N.Y.: Kehot, 1990), pp. 224-225.

4. On the Four Worlds, see Rabbi Yechiel Bar-Lev, *Song of the Soul,* pp. 57-65, 134. He points out that the World of Emanation is not separated from Divinity, whereas the other three Worlds have "screens," which limit the light and revelation of God. In the World of Emanation, there is nothing but the Ten *Sefirot*, which are completely united with the Infinite. In the World of Creation, which is a world of thought, the entire detailed plan of the universe exists. This level is also the source of souls. In the World of Formation are found angels and the various spiritual forces that give form to creation. In the World of Action is the material universe in which we live.

   These Worlds represent levels of Divine "concealment." Rabbi Bar-Lev compares levels of concealment in the universe to an electric current:

   > This current leaves the power plant in thick cables marked 'high voltage.' From there, the current is subdivided and reaches factories, large and small plants, and dwellings. In factories, there are machines whose electrical

requirements are quite high. Thus the electric company builds special equipment to regulate the electric current so that it reaches these factories at higher voltages, while it reaches homes at lower voltages. From this high voltage wire to the home this current passes *tzimtzumim* (limitations) through specially designed transformers....Similarly, light emerging from the *En Sof* [Infinite] is so lofty that it needs to pass through endless limitations until it is ready to be revealed, able to be conceived by creatures. We are not speaking only of humanity, but also of lofty creatures such as angels, seraphs and holy beings. (pp. 54-55)

5. Most philosophical discussions of the soul come from medieval times and subsequent eras but, as Rabbi Eliyahu Dessler observes, the Talmud also alludes to the need to attend to one's soul. The Sages clearly indicate that if we pursue illusory pleasures in this life, we will pursue them after death as well. He illustrates from a discussion reported in the Talmud between two souls who only want to see what everyone is doing and chatter about trivialities (*Berachot* 18b). The opposite fate is that of souls who work on themselves in this life: "Those who during their lifetime are attached to true spirituality will now experience fullness of being: 'Those who love Me will inherit Being' (Proverbs 8:21)." The lives of such people are fully complete within themselves because they are deeply connected with their souls, so they do not depend on externals, and they are happy with their lives. See *Strive for Truth!* Part 4 (New York: Feldheim, 1994), pp. 87-88.

6. Research on near-death experiences is reported in Raymond Moody, *Life After Life* (Marietta, Ga: Mockingbird Books, 1975) and his *Reflections on Life after Life* (New York: Bantam Books, 1977); Melvin Morse, *Parting Visions: Uses and Meanings of Pre-Death, Psychic and Spiritual Experiences* (New York: Random House, 1994); Melvin Morse with Paul Perry, *Transformed by the Light: The Powerful Effect of Near-Death Experiences on People's Lives* (New York: Random House, 1992); and P.M.H. Atwater, *Beyond the Light: What Isn't Being Said About Near-Death Experiences* (New York: Birch Lane Press, 1994).

7. See Rachel Noam, *The View from Above* (Lakewood, N.J.: CIS Press, 1992).

8. See for example, Dr. Brian Weiss, *Many Lives, Many Masters* (New York: Simon & Schuster, 1988); and his *Through Time Into Healing* (New York, NY: Simon & Schuster, 1992); Dr. Adrian Finkelstein, *Your Past Lives and the Healing Process* (Malibu, Calif.: 50 Gates Publishing, 1996). While these mention the soul world between incarnations, specific work in that area has come primarily from Michael Newton, *Journey of Souls: Case Studies of Life Between Lives* (St. Paul, Minn.: Llewellyn Publications, 1995).

9. The quotation is from Luzzatto, *Way of God,* 125. The Baal Shem Tov could often explain, to parents of a child who died, why he or she had been so ready to return to the world of souls. Rabbi Isaac Luria, the person who most clearly shaped modern Jewish mysticism, taught that the various generations of people described in the

Bible as meeting a bad fate (such as the generation of the Flood, or the generation that built the Tower of Babel) were each reincarnations of souls that had been born to Adam and Eve after they had been expelled from the Garden of Eden. Eventually, these souls were reincarnated again at the time of the Egyptian slavery and they had the opportunity to be redeemed. See Chaim Kramer, "Additional Notes on the Exodus," *The Breslov Hagaddah* (Jerusalem: Breslov Research Institute, 1992).

It is important to realize that reincarnation has been accepted among many Jewish scholars and has not necessarily been confined to esoteric circles of mystics or to popular hasidic tales. The Gaon of Vilna (Rabbi Eliyahu Kramer, 1720-1797), the outstanding scholar of his generation and an opponent of the Hasidim, explained that one's deeds in previous incarnations influence the kind of body in which one is reincarnated. For a full discussion, see Neil Gillman, *The Death of Death: Resurrection and Immortality in Jewish Thought* (Woodstock, Vt.: Jewish Lights, 1997), Chapter 7.

10. Rabbi Abraham Isaac Kook, "Lights from Darkness," section 32, *Orot,* p. 142.

11. The *sefirot* appear in various forms in early mystical texts, but became central to mystical thought after the appearance of the *Zohar* in the thirteenth century. The system was elucidated more fully by Rabbi Isaac Luria in the sixteenth century. His understanding of the *sefirot* is reflected in most books about Kabbalah available today.

One of the most lucid and complete explanations of the Sefirot in English is that of Rabbi Yechiel Bar-Lev, *Song of the Soul,* cited above. As Rabbi Bar-Lev explains, the *sefirot* are the original emanations from God, and constitute the World of Emanation *(Atzilut)*. Kabbalistic tradition describes them as the "roots" of everything that exists. Everything is a manifestation of the different sefirotic energies in some combination.

The human being also represents the map of cosmic energies in the form of the *sefirot*. As Rabbi Bar-Lev points out, "The entire universe may be seen as a mirror of man's physiognomy. All that exists in the universe exists in man; man is therefore described as a 'miniature world,' and the entire world is called 'man': *'adam d'briya, adam d'yetzira, adam d'asiya'* (i.e., man of creation, formation and making)" (*Song of the Soul,* p. 48). The contemporary term that most precisely captures this idea of the human being as a miniature world is "hologram."

12. Regarding the map of *sefirot* on the body: The theoretician of body work, Jeffrey Mishlove, has observed that maps of energy such as the Indian *chakras* and Chinese acupuncture systems are not precisely physical. Rather, they metaphorically and symbolically represent aspects of the body and soul. See Mishlove's *The Roots of Consciousness: The Classic Encyclopedia of Consciousness Studies* (Tulsa, Okla.: Council Oaks Books, 1993).

The system of *sefirot* has some elements in common with other systems. Some of the *sefirot* correspond to *chakra* points; however, where the *chakras* focus attention on points along the spine, the *sefirot* use a system of triangles. The triangle is the most stable geometric figure, and it can also be imagined three-dimensionally, as the outline of a cone. On the body, these "cones" of energy nest inside each other and replicate themselves on different levels.

In addition, the outer points of the triangles outline right and left "pillars," masculine and feminine respectively. These correspond to the yin/yang (right/left) division of the body in Chinese acupuncture, but the gender attributions are reversed; in the Chinese system, left is male and right female.

13. Following are the biblical references to the stories referred to in the sections of the *sefirot* of Emotion, Action, and Receptivity:

   ☐ Abraham: Midrash to Genesis 18:1-3.

   ☐ Ruth: The biblical Book of Ruth.

   ☐ Isaac: Genesis 22, 26-27, 35:27.

   ☐ Devorah: Judges 4-5; Hulda: 2 Kings 14: 20. These women were two of the seven female prophets whose prophecies were preserved in the Bible: Sarah, Miriam, Devorah, Channah, Abigail, Huldah, and Esther.

   ☐ Jacob: His story is spread over several chapters in Genesis, notably 25, 27-35, 45:25-47:10.

   ☐ Sarah: Her beauty and power, Genesis 12:14-20 (see Rashi on 12:17); the incident with Hagar, 21:9.

   ☐ Moses: Throughout the books of Exodus, Leviticus, Numbers, and Deuteronomy; the war with Amalek is in Exodus 17:8-16.

   ☐ Miriam: Exodus plus midrash; Song of the Sea is in 15:1-21; drying up of well, Number 20:1-4, with Rashi's commentary.

   ☐ Aaron: Throughout the books of Exodus, Leviticus, and Numbers.

   ☐ Abigail: 1 Samuel 25.

   ☐ Joseph: Genesis 37, 39-47, his encounter with Potiphar's wife in 39:10-12.

   ☐ Boaz: The Book of Ruth.

   ☐ Tamar: Genesis 38.

   ☐ Judith: The Book of Judith (an extra-biblical book, usually included in collections of readings for Chanukkah).

   ☐ David: 1 and 2 Samuel.

14. The term *Mashiach* or Messiah means "anointed one," that is, selected by God; Moses is also considered a Messianic figure, but he did not establish a kingdom in the Land.

15. Since ancient times, the Jewish Sages have recognized that ego—which they usually called "arrogance" or "vanity"—is the chief obstacle to spiritual growth. "Rav Sula said, 'Every arrogant person will eventually sin.'....Rav Nachman said, 'It is evi-

dent that an arrogant person is one who has already sinned'" (*Taanis* 7b). Rabbenu Bachya wrote in *Duties of the Heart,* a medieval tract, "If you do not find defects within yourself, I am afraid you have the greatest defect of all—vanity."

On the other hand, the person who is humble can achieve spiritual greatness, like Moses, whom the Torah extolled for his humility. "A man grows humble," wrote the Lubavitcher Rebbe, "when he realizes that Godliness is the true essence of all being." See Rabbi Menachem Mendel Schneerson, *Chassidic Dimension,* Vol. 1, p. 161. Rabbi Aryeh Kaplan made the same point poetically when he wrote, "When a person is ready to replace his ego with a question, then he is ready to be reborn with its answer." *See The Aryeh Kaplan Anthology,* Vol. 2 (New York: Mesorah Publications, 1991), p. 322.

16. On purifying the body through performing the commandments, see Luzzatto, *Knowing Heart,* p. 107. The ideas of "purification" and its opposite, "defilement," are somewhat foreign to modern culture. Rabbi Menachem Mendel Schneerson explained defilement as being the result of a weakening of our bonds with God through our sins. When we weaken those bonds (or do not continue to strengthen them), we are less alive. We have a touch of death, which produces defilement. When we return to God, we refine or purify ourselves (through Godly action). See *Chassidic Dimension,* Vol. 1, p. 200.

17. For information about colors and *sefirot,* see Aryeh Kaplan, *Meditation and Kabbalah* (York Beach, Maine: Samuel Weiser, 1982), p. 181; and Glazerson, *Torah, Light and Healing,* pp. 87-89. The *Zohar* and other sources use slightly different color systems from the one suggested here, and those differ in some respects from the Indian *chakra* color system which is essentially a rainbow arrangement.

Chapter 6

1. Rabbi Schneur Zalman of Liadi, *"Sefer Shel Benonim,"* in *Sefer Likutei Amarim—Tanya,* Chapter 23, p. 95.

2. This phenomenon, known today as "projection," was well known to our classic commentators as well. Rashi observes on Deuteronomy 1:27 that, while the Jewish people claimed that God hated them, they were really assuming that their own ill-will was God's emotion.

3. Rabbi Elchanan Tauber's lectures, May-June, 1996, Los Angeles, California, provided this analogy for understanding *Malkhut.*

4. On colors used in visualization, see Chapter 5, note 17.

Glossary

Where appropriate, the literal meaning of the Hebrew is translated in quotations immediately after the word or phrase cited.

Aron HaKodesh: The ark in which the Torah scrolls are kept in a synagogue.

Asher Yatzar: "Who creates..." The blessing of thanks for the body, said in the morning and after relieving oneself.

Asiyah: "Action." The fourth and lowest of the Four Worlds according to *Kabbalah,* namely, the world of action and material form.

Atzilut: "Emanation." The first and highest of the Four Worlds according to Kabbalah, in which God began creating the world by emanating Divine energy.

Baal Shem Tov: Israel ben Eliezer (1698-1760). "Master of the Good Name." The founder of Hasidism in Eastern Europe, famous for his tales, mystical feats and soul-travels, and parables explaining the Torah.

Beit HaMikdash: "House of the Holy One." The Temple in Jerusalem that existed from the time of Solomon until its destruction by the Babylonian army in 586 B.C.E. It began to be rebuilt about 70 years later, and became again the center of Jewish worship until its destruction by the Romans in 70 C.E.

Beriah: "Creation." The second of the Four Worlds according to *Kabbalah,* where God's energy began to take the form of thoughts. This world is the root source of human souls.

Binah: "Understanding." One of the *sefirot* of thought, involving the function of nourishing and allowing a thought to develop and be related to other thoughts.

Bircat Ha-Shachar: "Morning Blessings." The section of prayers said upon arising, usually repeated in synagogue services for the benefit of those who have not said them.

Bircat HaTorah: "Blessings of the Torah." Section of the Morning Blessings said over Torah study; also, blessings said over being called to the Torah in synagogue.

Cohanim: "Priests." Historically, the segment of the tribe of Levi descended from Aaron, assigned to the most holy service in the *Mishkan* and, later, the Temple in Jerusalem.

Daat: "Knowledge." One of the *sefirot* of thought, with the quality of being able to internalize knowledge by connecting the mind with the emotions.

Dam: "Blood." Carrier of the life of the soul within the body. It includes, according to Jewish healing traditions, not only the red fluid known to us as "blood" but also the lymphatic system and the electrical current of the nervous system.

Elohai Neshamah: "My God, the soul..." One of the Morning Blessings, giving thanks for the soul.

Elu Devarim: "These are the things..." A section of the Oral Torah read after the *Bircat HaTorah*, specifying some of the important *mitzvot.*

Gemara: The written collections of rabbinic discussions (ca. 200-600 C.E.) of the laws covered in the Mishnah. Together with the Mishnah, the Gemara constitutes the principal content of the Talmud.

Gevurah: "Strength." One of the *sefirot* of emotions, with the qualities of restraint, discipline, and inner strength.

Guf: "Body."

Halachah: "The walking." The tradition of Jewish law.

Hasidism: A popular Jewish religious movement that began in late-eighteenth-century Eastern Europe, fully within the Orthodox framework, emphasizing devotion in prayer, love of one's fellow, and strong relationships between teacher *(rebbe)* and disciple *(hasid)*. Hasidic rebbes were noted for their ability to transmit difficult concepts of Jewish mysticism to the ordinary person.

Chesed: "Lovingkindness." One of the *sefirot* of emotions, with the quality of devoted love for another person.

Hod: "Glory." One of the *sefirot* of action, emphasizing the quality of stability and balance. Related to the word *todah,* which means thanksgiving.

Chochmah: "Wisdom." One of the *sefirot* of thought, with the ability to receive and transmit a spark of new insight.

Holy of Holies: The section of the *Mishkan* (or Temple) where only the *Cohain Gadol* (the High Priest) was permitted to enter, and then only on Yom Kippur.

Kabbalah: Generally, the Jewish mystical tradition. Its written works go back, depending on how one dates the texts, to either the second or the fifth centuries C.E.

Kelipot: (singular *kelipah*) "Husks." A term from Kabbalah signifying the evil forces in the world, which are portrayed as shells or husks that cover the sparks of Divine light that are in every created thing.

Keruvim: "Cherubim." The angelic figures made of beaten gold on top of the cover of the ark containing the *luchot*, in the *Mishkan* (and later the Temple).

Luchot: The tablets of the Law given to Moses, on which were engraved the Ten Commandments.

Mah Tovu: "How good [fair]..." One of the prayers in the Morning Blessings, composed of scriptural selections, expressing thanks for being in a place where one can worship.

Malkhut: "Kingship." The tenth of the *sefirot*, expressing the full manifestation of the soul in the material world.

Megillah: "Scroll." Usually refers to *Megillat Esther,* the Scroll of Esther read at Purim. The term may also refer to a scroll read on certain other holidays.

Midrash: The general term for the collections of homiletic and inspirational scriptural interpretation, particularly using stories and word-associations, produced during the third to eighth centuries C.E.

Mishkan: "Dwelling Place." The portable sanctuary constructed by the Israelites according to the instructions and vision given to Moses shortly after the revelation at Sinai. This sanctuary was used during the desert travels and was set up in several successive locations once the people reached the land of Israel, finally coming to rest in Solomon's temple.

Mishnah: The primary written collection of rabbinic explanations of the laws of the Torah. Several "mishnahs" were collected in the late first and second century C.E., but the collection that became definitive was made by Rabbi Judah Ha-Levi toward the end of the second century. The Mishnah forms the core for later Talmudic discussions, which are known as Gemara. Both Mishnah and Gemara are included in any edition of the Talmud.

Mitzvah: "Commandment."

Modeh Ani: "I give thanks..." The first prayer said in the morning, thanking God for restoring the soul to the body.

Nefesh: A biblical term for the soul, used in later writings to mean the aspect of the soul that vitalizes the physical body.

Neshamah: A biblical term for the soul, used in later writings to mean the aspect of the soul most directly connected to the mind; also, popularly, for the essence of a person.

Netzach: "Victory." One of the *sefirot* of action, expressing perseverance and motion.

Pesuke d'Zimra: "Verses of Song." A section of the morning prayer service, following the *Bircat HaShachar.*

Ruach: A biblical term for the soul, usually translated as "spirit," and also meaning "wind." In later writings, *ruach* is the aspect of the soul most closely connected with the emotions and motivation.

Sefirot: (singular: *Sefirah*). The ten Divine energies manifested in every process of creation.

Shemoneh Esreh: "Eighteen [Blessings]." The high point of the morning prayer service, said almost silently while standing, in which petitions to God are said.

Siddur: "Order." The Jewish prayerbook.

Talmud: The records of extensive discussions of Jewish sages on topics of Jewish law, from the third to the sixth centuries, which form the textual core of Judaism from that time onward. While Talmuds were collected and edited in both the Babylonian and Israelite communities, the word "Talmud" usually refers to the Babylonian Talmud (the other being the less comprehensive Jerusalem Talmud).

Tanya: "It has been taught..." The first word and the common title of the *Sefer Shel Benonim* or "Book for the Average Person," written by Rabbi Schneur Zalman of Liadi in the early nineteenth century. It became a classic of Hasidic philosophy and practical teachings on prayer, not only for Rabbi Schneur Zalman's group, Chabad-Lubavitch, but for many other Hasidim as well. Today, it is universally recognized as a great work on spiritual self-improvement.

Tiferet: "Harmony." One of the *sefirot* of emotions, expressing a balance between lovingkindness and discipline, and also the quality of inner truth.

Yesod: "Foundation." One of the *sefirot* of action, with the quality of channeling of powerful passions into creative activity.

Yetzirah: "Formation." The third of the Four Worlds of Kabbalah, denoting the stage of creation in which things were given their distinct qualities of energy.

Recommended Readings

Bar-Lev, Rabbi Yechiel. *Song of the Soul: Introduction to Kaballa.* (Originally published in English under the title *Yedid Nefesh.*) Petach Tikva, Israel, n.p.: 1994.

Donin, Rabbi Hayim Halevy. *To Pray as a Jew: A Guide to the Prayer Book and the Synagogue Service.* New York: Basic Books, 1980.

Frankel, Avraham Yaakov. *In My Flesh I See God: A Treasury of Rabbinic Insights About the Human Anatomy.* Northvale, N.J.: Jason Aronson, 1995.

Gillman, Neil. *The Death of Death: Resurrection and Immortality in Jewish Thought.* Woodstock, Vt.: Jewish Lights, 1997.

Glazerson, Matityahu. *Torah, Light and Healing: Mystical Insights into Healing, Based on the Hebrew Language.* Jerusalem: Lev Eliahu, 1993.

Goldberger, Rabbi Moshe, et al., *Singing Hashem's Praises: Lessons from the Organs of the Body.* Staten Island, N.Y.: 1987.

Green, Arthur, and Barry W. Holtz, eds *Your Word Is Fire: The Hasidic Masters on Contemplative Prayer*, ed. Woodstock, Vt.: Jewish Lights, 1993.

Greenbaum, Avraham. *Wings of the Sun: Traditional Jewish Healing in Theory and Practice.* Jerusalem: Breslov Research Institute, 1995.

Kook, Rabbi Abraham Isaac. *Orot* (1920), Translated by Bezalel Naor (Northvale, N.J.: Jason Aronson, 1993).

_____. *The Lights of Penitence, the Moral Principles, Lights of Holiness, Essays, Letters, and Poems.* Translated by Ben Zion Bokser. New York: Paulist Press, 1978.

Luzzatto, Rabbi Moshe Chaim (the RaMChaL). *The Knowing Heart: The Philosophy of God's Oneness.* Translated by Shraga Silverstein. New York: Feldheim, 1982.

_____. *The Way of God.* Translated and annotated by Rabbi Aryeh Kaplan. Fourth edition. New York: Feldheim, 1983.

Miller, Rabbi Avigdor. *The Beginning: Comments and Notes on Breshis.* New York: Avigdor Miller, 1987.

_____. *A Kingdom of Cohanim: Commentary and Notes on Vayikra.* New York: Avigdor Miller, 1994.

Mindel, Rabbi Nissan. *As for Me—My Prayer: A Commentary on the Daily Prayers.* Brooklyn, N.Y.: Merkos L'Inyonei Chinuch, 1984.

Munk, Rabbi Elie. *The World of Prayer.* 2 vols. New York: Philip Feldheim, 1987.

Nachman of Breslov, Rabbi. *Likutey Moharan,* 3 vols. Vol. 1 trans. by Simcha Bergman; Vols. 2 & 3 trans. by Moshe Mykoff; annot. Chaim Kramer. New York: Breslov Research Institute, 1986-1990.

Noam, Rachel. *The View from Above.* Lakewood, N.J.: CIS Press, 1992.

Scherman, Rabbi Nosson. Commentary to *Siddur Kol Yaakov* (Ashkenaz), second edition. Brooklyn, N.Y.: Mesorah Publications, 1986.

Schneerson, Rabbi Menachem Mendel. *The Chassidic Dimension,* Vol. 1. Compiled by Rabbi Sholom B. Wineberg and edited by Uri Kaploun. Brooklyn, N.Y.: Kehot Publication Society, 1990.

_____. *Likutei Sichot: An Anthology of Talks.* Brooklyn, N.Y.: Kehot Publication Society, 1992.

Schneur Zalman of Liadi, Rabbi. *Likutei Amarim: Tanya.* Brooklyn, N.Y.: Kehot Publication Society, 1981.

Steinsaltz, Rabbi Adin. *The Thirteen Petaled Rose.* New York: Basic Books, 1980.

Weintraub, Simkha Y., ed. *Healing of Soul, Healing of Body: Spiritual Leaders Unfold the Strength & Solace in Psalms.* Woodstock, Vt.: Jewish Lights Publishing, 1994.

About JEWISH LIGHTS Publishing

People of all faiths and backgrounds yearn for books that attract, engage, educate and spiritually inspire.

Our principal goal is to stimulate thought and help all people learn about who the Jewish People are, where they come from, and what the future can be made to hold. While people of our diverse Jewish heritage are the primary audience, our books speak to people in the Christian world as well and will broaden their understanding of Judaism and the roots of their own faith.

We bring to you authors who are at the forefront of spiritual thought and experience. While each has something different to say, they all say it in a voice that you can hear.

Our books are designed to welcome you and then to engage, stimulate and inspire. We judge our success not only by whether or not our books are beautiful and commercially successful, but by whether or not they make a difference in your life.

We at Jewish Lights take great care to produce beautiful books that present meaningful spiritual content in a form that reflects the art of making high quality books. Therefore, we want to acknowledge those who contributed to the production of this book.

EDITORIAL & PROOFREADING
Sandra Korinchak

PRODUCTION
Maria O'Donnell

BOOK & COVER DESIGN
Chelsea Dippel, Scotia, New York

TYPE
Set in Esprit
Chelsea Dippel, Scotia, New York

HEBREW TYPESETTING
Joel Hoffman, Rye, New York
Peggy Davis, Colrain, Massachusetts

ART
Michael Heffernan, South Woodstock, Vermont
Pam Wasserman, Woodstock, Vermont

COVER PRINTING
Phoenix Color Corp., Hingham, Massachusetts

PRINTING AND BINDING
Hamilton Printing, Castleton, New York

MINDING THE TEMPLE OF THE SOUL
Audiotape of the Prayers, Movements & Meditations
by Judy Greenfeld and Tamar Frankiel

This audiotape enhances the spiritual workout offered in *Minding the Temple of the Soul*. It contains the blessings, the meditations and movements which accompany them, and the additional meditations found throughout the book.

MTAPE   1 cassette, 60 min. **$9.95**

Videotape of the Blessings & Meditations

VHS 0 @507, 46 min. **$20.00**

JEWISH LIGHTS Publishing
P.O. Box 237 • Sunset Farm Offices, Rte. 4
Woodstock, Vermont 05091
Tel (802) 457-4000   Fax (802) 457-4004   www.jewishlights.com

Toll free credit card orders (800) 962-4544 (9-5 ET M-F)

Spirituality

MEDITATION FROM THE HEART OF JUDAISM
Today's Teachers Share Their Practices, Techniques, and Faith
Ed. by *Avram Davis*

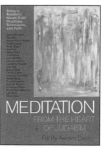

A "how to" guide for both beginning and experienced meditators, *Meditation from the Heart of Judaism* will help you start meditating or help you enhance your practice.

Here, in their own individual voices, 22 masters of meditation—rabbis, scholars, psychologists, teachers—explain why and how they meditate. *A detailed compendium of the experts' "Best Practices"* offers practical advice, starting points, and—most of all—direction for making meditation a source of spiritual energy in our own lives.

"A treasury of meditative insights and techniques....Each page is a meditative experience that brings you closer to God."
—*Rabbi Shoni Labowitz, author of* Miraculous Living: A Guided Journey in Kabbalah

6" x 9", 256 pp. Hardcover, ISBN 1-879045-77-X **$21.95**

SELF, STRUGGLE & CHANGE
Family Conflict Stories in Genesis and Their Healing Insights for Our Lives
by *Norman J. Cohen*

How do I find greater wholeness in my life and in my family's life?

The stress of late-20th-century living only brings new variations to timeless personal struggles. The people described by the biblical writers of Genesis were in situations and relationships very much like our own. We identify with them. Their stories still speak to us because they are about the same problems we deal with every day.

A modern master of biblical interpretation brings us greater understanding of the ancient text and of ourselves in this intriguing re-telling of conflict between husband and wife, father and son, brothers, and sisters.

"Delightfully written ... rare erudition, sensitivity and insight."
— *Elie Wiesel*

6" x 9", 224 pp. Quality Paperback, ISBN 1-879045-66-4 **$16.95**; Hardcover, ISBN -19-2 **$21.95**

ECOLOGY & THE JEWISH SPIRIT
Where Nature and the Sacred Meet
Ed. and with Introductions by *Ellen Bernstein*

What is nature's place in our spiritual lives?

A focus on nature is part of the fabric of Jewish thought. Here, experts bring us a richer understanding of the long-neglected themes of nature that are woven through the biblical creation story, ancient texts, traditional law, the holiday cycles, prayer, *mitzvot* (good deeds), and community.

For people of all faiths, all backgrounds, this book helps us to make nature a sacred, spiritual part of our own lives.

"A great resource for anyone seeking to explore the connection between their faith and caring for God's good creation, our environment."
—*Paul Gorman, Executive Director, National Religious Partnership for the Environment*

6" x 9", 288 pp, Hardcover, ISBN 1-879045-88-5 **$23.95**

Spirituality

HOW TO BE A PERFECT STRANGER, In 2 Volumes
A Guide to Etiquette in Other People's Religious Ceremonies
Edited by Stuart M. Matlins & Arthur J. Magida

"A book that belongs in every living room, library and office!"

Explains the rituals and celebrations of America's major religions/denominations, helping an interested guest to feel comfortable, participate to the fullest extent possible, and avoid violating anyone's religious principles. Answers practical questions from the perspective of *any* other faith.

VOL. 1: America's Largest Faiths

VOL. 1 COVERS: Assemblies of God • Baptist • Buddhist • Christian Science • Churches of Christ • Disciples of Christ • Episcopalian • Greek Orthodox • Hindu • Islam • Jehovah's Witnesses • Jewish • Lutheran • Methodist • Mormon • Presbyterian • Quaker • Roman Catholic • Seventh-day Adventist • United Church of Christ

6" x 9", 432 pp. Hardcover, ISBN 1-879045-39-7 **$24.95**

VOL. 2: Other Faiths in America

VOL. 2 COVERS: African American Methodist Churches • Baha'i • Christian and Missionary Alliance • Christian Congregation • Church of the Brethren • Church of the Nazarene • Evangelical Free Church of America • International Church of the Foursquare Gospel • International Pentecostal Holiness Church • Mennonite/Amish • Native American • Orthodox Churches • Pentecostal Church of God • Reformed Church of America • Sikh • Unitarian Universalist • Wesleyan

6" x 9", 416 pp. Hardcover, ISBN 1-879045-63-X **$24.95**

GOD & THE BIG BANG
Discovering Harmony Between Science & Spirituality
by *Daniel C. Matt*

Mysticism and science: What do they have in common? How can one enlighten the other? By drawing on modern cosmology and ancient Kabbalah, Matt shows how science and religion can together enrich our spiritual awareness and help us recover a sense of wonder and find our place in the universe.

"This poetic new book...helps us to understand the human meaning of creation."
—*Joel Primack, leading cosmologist, Professor of Physics, University of California, Santa Cruz*

6" x 9", 216 pp. Hardcover, ISBN 1-879045-48-6 **$21.95**

MINDING THE TEMPLE OF THE SOUL
Balancing Body, Mind & Spirit through Traditional Jewish Prayer, Movement & Meditation
by *Tamar Frankiel* and *Judy Greenfeld*

This new spiritual approach to physical health introduces readers to a spiritual tradition that affirms the body and enables them to reconceive their bodies in a more positive light. Relying on Kabbalistic teachings and other Jewish traditions, it shows us how to be more responsible for our own psychological and physical health. Focuses on the discipline of prayer, simple Tai Chi-like exercises and body positions, and guides the reader throughout, step by step, with diagrams, sketches and meditations.

7" x 10", 184 pp, Quality Paperback Original, illus., ISBN 1-879045-64-8 **$16.95**

Audiotape of the Prayers, Movements & Meditations (60-min. cassette) **$9.95**
Videotape of the Blessings & Meditations (46-min. VHS) **$20.00**

Healing/Recovery/Wellness

Experts Praise *Twelve Jewish Steps to Recovery*

"Recommended reading for people of all denominations."
—*Rabbi Abraham J. Twerski, M.D.*

TWELVE JEWISH STEPS TO RECOVERY
A Personal Guide to Turning from Alcoholism & Other Addictions...Drugs, Food, Gambling, Sex...
by *Rabbi Kerry M. Olitzky & Stuart A. Copans, M.D.*
Preface by *Abraham J. Twerski, M.D.*; Intro. by *Rabbi Sheldon Zimmerman* "Getting Help" by *JACS Foundation*

A Jewish perspective on the Twelve Steps of addiction recovery programs with consolation, inspiration and motivation for recovery. It draws from traditional sources and quotes from what recovering Jewish people say about their experiences with addictions of all kinds. Inspiring illustrations of the twelve gates of the Old City of Jerusalem.

6" x 9", 136 pp. Quality Paperback, ISBN 1-879045-09-5 **$13.95**

Recovery from Codependence: A Jewish Twelve Steps Guide to Healing Your Soul
by Dr. Kerry M. Olitzky

6" x 9", 160 pp. Quality Paperback Original, ISBN 1-879045-32-X **$13.95** HC, ISBN -27-3 **$21.95**

Renewed Each Day: Daily Twelve Step Recovery Meditations Based on the Bible
by Dr. Kerry M. Olitzky & Aaron Z.

6" x 9", Quality Paperback Original, **V. I**, 224 pp. **$12.95** **V. II**, 280 pp. **$14.95**
Two-Volume Set ISBN 1-879045-21-4 **$27.90**

One Hundred Blessings Every Day: Daily Twelve Step Recovery Affirmations, Exercises for Personal Growth & Renewal Reflecting Seasons of the Jewish Year
by Dr. Kerry M. Olitzky

4 1/2" x 6 1/2", 432 pp. Quality Paperback Original, ISBN 1-879045-30-3 **$14.95**

HEALING OF SOUL, HEALING OF BODY
Spiritual Leaders Unfold the Strength and Solace in Psalms
Edited by *Rabbi Simkha Y. Weintraub, CSW, for The Jewish Healing Center*

A source of solace for those who are facing illness, as well as those who care for them. The ten Psalms which form the core of this healing resource were originally selected 200 years ago by Rabbi Nachman of Breslov as a "complete remedy." Today, for anyone coping with illness, they continue to provide a wellspring of strength. Each Psalm is newly translated, making it clear and accessible, and each one is introduced by an eminent rabbi, men and women reflecting different movements and backgrounds. To all who are living with the pain and uncertainty of illness, this spiritual resource offers an anchor of spiritual comfort.

"Will bring comfort to anyone fortunate enough to read it. This gentle book is a luminous gem of wisdom."
—*Larry Dossey, M.D., author of* Healing Words: The Power of Prayer & the Practice of Medicine

6" x 9", 128 pp. Quality Paperback Original, illus., 2-color text, ISBN 1-879045-31-1 **$14.95**

Spirituality

MY PEOPLE'S PRAYER BOOK
Traditional Prayers, Modern Commentaries
Vol. 1—The Sh'ma and Its Blessings
Edited by Rabbi Lawrence A. Hoffman

My People's Prayer Book provides a diverse and exciting commentary to the traditional liturgy, written by 10 of today's most respected scholars and teachers from all perspectives of the Jewish world.

The groundbreaking first volume examines the oldest and best-known of Jewish prayers. Often the first prayer memorized by children and the last prayer recited on a deathbed, the *Sh'ma* frames a Jewish life.

7" x 10", 168 pp. Hardcover, ISBN 1-879045-79-6 **$19.95**

FINDING JOY
A Practical Spiritual Guide to Happiness
by *Dannel I. Schwartz* with *Mark Hass*

Searching for happiness in our modern world of stress and struggle is common; *finding* it is more unusual. This guide explores and explains how to find joy through a time-honored, creative—and surprisingly practical—approach based on the teachings of Jewish mysticism and Kabbalah.

"This lovely, simple introduction to Kabbalah....is a singular contribution to *tikkun olam*, repairing the world."
—*American Library Association's* Booklist

•AWARD WINNER•

6" x 9", 192 pp. Hardcover, ISBN 1-879045-53-2 **$19.95**

THE DEATH OF DEATH
Resurrection and Immortality in Jewish Thought
by *Neil Gillman*

Noted theologian Neil Gillman explores the original and compelling argument that Judaism, a religion often thought to pay little attention to the afterlife, not only offers us rich ideas on the subject—but delivers a deathblow to death itself. By exploring Jewish thought about death and the afterlife, this fascinating work presents us with challenging new ideas about our lives.

"Enables us to recover our tradition's understanding of the afterlife and breaks through the silence of modern Jewish thought on immortality.... A work of major significance."
—*Rabbi Sheldon Zimmerman, President, Hebrew Union College–Jewish Institute of Religion*

6" x 9", 336 pp, Hardcover, ISBN 1-879045-61-3 **$23.95**

THE EMPTY CHAIR: FINDING HOPE & JOY
Timeless Wisdom from a Hasidic Master,
Rebbe Nachman of Breslov
Adapted by Moshe Mykoff and the Breslov Research Institute

A "little treasure" of aphorisms and advice for living joyously and spiritually today, written 200 years ago, but startlingly fresh in meaning and use. Challenges and helps us to move from stress and sadness to hope and joy.

Teacher, guide and spiritual master—Rebbe Nachman provides vital words of inspiration and wisdom for life today for people of any faith, or of no faith.

AWARD WINNER

"For anyone of any faith, this is a book of healing and wholeness, of being alive!"
— *Bookviews*

4" x 6", 128 pp., 2-color text, Deluxe Paperback, ISBN 1-879045-67-2 **$9.95**

Spirituality—The Kushner Series

INVISIBLE LINES OF CONNECTION
Sacred Stories of the Ordinary
by *Lawrence Kushner*

Through his everyday encounters with family, friends, colleagues and strangers, Kushner takes us deeply into our lives, finding flashes of spiritual insight in the process. This is a book where literature meets spirituality, where the sacred meets the ordinary, and, above all, where people of all faiths, all backgrounds can meet one another and themselves.

•AWARD WINNER•

"Does something both more and different than instruct—it inspirits. Wonderful stories, from the best storyteller I know."
— *David Mamet*

5 1/2" x 8 1/2", 160 pp. Hardcover, ISBN 1-879045-52-4 **$21.95**

HONEY FROM THE ROCK
An Easy Introduction to Jewish Mysticism
by *Lawrence Kushner*

"Quite simply the easiest introduction to Jewish mysticism you can read."

An introduction to the ten gates of Jewish mysticism and how it applies to daily life.

"Captures the flavor and spark of Jewish mysticism. . . . Read it and be rewarded." —*Elie Wiesel*

6" x 9", 168 pp. Quality Paperback, ISBN 1-879045-02-8 **$14.95**

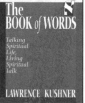

THE BOOK OF WORDS
Talking Spiritual Life, Living Spiritual Talk
by *Lawrence Kushner*

In the incomparable manner of his extraordinary *The Book of Letters*, Kushner now lifts up and shakes the dust off primary religious words we use to describe the spiritual dimension of life. For each word Kushner offers us a startling, moving and insightful explication, and pointed readings from classical Jewish sources that further illuminate the concept. He concludes with a short exercise that helps unite the spirit of the word with our actions in the world.

"This is a powerful and holy book."
—*M. Scott Peck, M.D., author of* The Road Less Traveled *and other books*

"What a delightful wholeness of intellectual vigor and meditative playfulness, and all in a tone of gentleness that speaks to this gentile."
—*Rt. Rev. Krister Stendahl, formerly Dean, Harvard Divinity School/Bishop of Stockholm*

6" x 9", 152 pp. Hardcover, beautiful two-color text ISBN 1-879045-35-4 **$21.95**

THE BOOK OF LETTERS
A Mystical Hebrew Alphabet
by *Rabbi Lawrence Kushner*

In calligraphy by the author. Folktales about and exploration of the mystical meanings of the Hebrew Alphabet. Open the old prayerbook-like pages of *The Book of Letters* and you will enter a special world of sacred tradition and religious feeling. Rabbi Kushner draws from ancient Judaic sources, weaving Talmudic commentary, Hasidic folktales, and Kabbalistic mysteries around the letters.

"A book which is in love with Jewish letters."
— *Isaac Bashevis Singer* (ל)

•AWARD WINNER•

• **Popular Hardcover Edition** 6"x 9", 80 pp. Hardcover, two colors, inspiring new Foreword. ISBN 1-879045-00-1 **$24.95**

• **Deluxe Gift Edition** 9"x 12", 80 pp. Hardcover, four-color text, ornamentation, in a beautiful slipcase. ISBN 1-879045-01-X **$79.95**

• **Collector's Limited Edition** 9"x 12", 80 pp. Hardcover, gold embossed pages, hand assembled slipcase. With silkscreened print. **Limited to 500 signed and numbered copies.** ISBN 1-879045-04-4 **$349.00**

To see a sample page at no obligation, call us

Spirituality

GOD WAS IN THIS PLACE & I, i DID NOT KNOW
Finding Self, Spirituality & Ultimate Meaning
by Lawrence Kushner

Who am I? Who is God? Kushner creates inspiring interpretations of Jacob's dream in Genesis, opening a window into Jewish spirituality for people of all faiths and backgrounds.

In this fascinating blend of scholarship, imagination, psychology and history, seven Jewish spiritual masters ask and answer fundamental questions of human experience.

"Rich and intriguing."
—*M. Scott Peck, M.D., author of* The Road Less Traveled *and other books*

6" x 9", 192 pp. Quality Paperback, ISBN 1-879045 33 8 **$16.95**

THE RIVER OF LIGHT
Spirituality, Judaism, Consciousness
by Lawrence Kushner

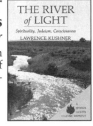

A "manual" for all spiritual travelers who would attempt a spiritual journey in our times. Taking us step by step, Kushner allows us to discover the meaning of our own quest: "to allow the river of light—the deepest currents of consciousness—to rise to the surface and animate our lives."

"Philosophy and mystical fantasy....Anybody—Jewish, Christian, or otherwise...will find this book an intriguing experience."
—*The Kirkus Reviews*

6" x 9", 180 pp. Quality Paperback, ISBN 1-879045-03-6 **$14.95**

GODWRESTLING—ROUND 2
Ancient Wisdom, Future Paths
by Arthur Waskow

BEST RELIGION BOOK OF THE YEAR

This 20th anniversary sequel to a seminal book of the Jewish renewal movement deals with spirituality in relation to personal growth, marriage, ecology, feminism, politics, and more. Including new chapters on recent issues and concerns, Waskow outlines original ways to merge "religious" life and "personal" life in our society today.

"A delicious read and a soaring meditation."
—*Rabbi Zalman M. Schachter-Shalomi*

"Vivid as a novel, sharp, eccentric, loud....An important book for anyone who wants to bring Judaism alive."
—*Marge Piercy*

6 x 9, 352 pp. Hardcover, ISBN 1-879045-45-1 **$23.95**

BEING GOD'S PARTNER
How to Find the Hidden Link Between Spirituality and Your Work
by Jeffrey K. Salkin Introduction by *Norman Lear*

A book that will challenge people of every denomination to reconcile the cares of work and soul. A groundbreaking book about spirituality and the work world, from a Jewish perspective. Helps the reader find God in the ethical striving and search for meaning in the professions and in business and offers practical suggestions for balancing your professional life and spiritual self.

"This engaging meditation on the spirituality of work is grounded in Judaism but is relevant well beyond the boundaries of that tradition."
—*Booklist (American Library Association)*

6" x 9", 192 pp. Quality Paperback, ISBN 1-879045-65-6 **$16.95** HC, ISBN -37-0 **$19.95**

Theology/Philosophy

ISRAEL
An Echo of Eternity
by *Abraham Joshua Heschel* with New Introduction by *Susannah Heschel*

In this classic reprint originally published by Farrar, Straus & Giroux, one of the foremost religious figures of our century gives us a powerful and eloquent statement on the meaning of Israel in our time. Heschel looks at the past, present and future home of the Jewish people. He tells us how and why the presence of Israel has tremendous historical and religious significance for the whole world.

5 1/2" x 8", 272 pp. Quality Paperback Original, ISBN 1-879045-70-2 **$18.95**

THE SPIRIT OF RENEWAL
Finding Faith After the Holocaust
by *Edward Feld*

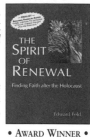

"Boldly redefines the landscape of Jewish religious thought after the Holocaust."
—*Rabbi Lawrence Kushner*

Trying to understand the Holocaust and addressing the question of faith after the Holocaust, Rabbi Feld explores three key cycles of destruction and recovery in Jewish history, each of which radically reshaped Jewish understanding of God, people, and the world.

• AWARD WINNER •

"A profound meditation on Jewish history [and the Holocaust]....Christians, as well as many others, need to share in this story."
—*The Rt. Rev. Frederick H. Borsch, Ph.D., Episcopal Bishop of L.A.*

6" x 9", 224 pp. Quality Paperback, ISBN 1-879045-40-0 **$16.95** HC, ISBN-06-0 **$22.95**

SEEKING THE PATH TO LIFE
Theological Meditations On God
and the Nature of People, Love, Life and Death
by *Rabbi Ira F. Stone*

For people who never thought they would read a book of theology—let alone understand it, enjoy it, savor it and have it affect the way they think about their lives. In 45 intense meditations, each a page or two in length, Stone takes us on explorations of the most basic human struggles: Life and death, love and anger, peace and war, covenant and exile.

• AWARD WINNER • "A bold book....The reader of any faith will be inspired...."
— *The Rev. Carla V. Berkedal, Episcopal Priest*

6" x 9", 132 pp. Quality Paperback, ISBN 1-879045-47-8 **$14.95** HC, ISBN-17-6 **$19.95**

THEOLOGY & PHILOSOPHY...Other books—Classic Reprints

Aspects of Rabbinic Theology by Solomon Schechter, with a new introduction by Neil Gillman 6" x 9", 440 pp, Quality Paperback, ISBN 1-879045-24-9 **$18.95**

The Earth Is the Lord's: The Inner World of the Jew in Eastern Europe by Abraham Joshua Heschel with woodcut illustrations by Ilya Schor
5 1/2" x 8", 112 pp, Quality Paperback, ISBN 1-879045-42-7 **$13.95**

Judaism & Modern Man: An Interpretation of Jewish Religion by Will Herberg; new introduction by Neil Gillman 5.5" x 8.5", 336 pp, Quality Paperback, ISBN 1-879045-87-7 **$18.95**

The Last Trial: On the Legends and Lore of the Command to Abraham to Offer Isaac as a Sacrifice by Shalom Spiegel, with a new introduction by Judah Goldin
6" x 9", 208 pp, Quality Paperback, ISBN 1-879045-29-X **$17.95**

A Passion for Truth: Despair and Hope in Hasidism by Abraham Joshua Heschel
5 1/2" x 8", 352 pp, Quality Paperback, ISBN 1-879045-41-9 **$18.95**

Tormented Master: The Life and Spiritual Quest of Rabbi Nahman of Bratslav by Arthur Green 6" x 9", 408 pp, Quality Paperback, ISBN 1-879045-11-7 **$18.95**

Your Word Is Fire Edited and translated with a new introduction by Arthur Green and Barry W. Holtz 6" x 9", 152 pp, Quality Paperback, ISBN 1-879045-25-7 **$14.95**

Life Cycle

MOURNING & MITZVAH
A Guided Journal for Walking the Mourner's Path Through Grief to Healing

• With over 60 guided exercises •

by *Anne Brener, L.C.S.W.*; Foreword by *Rabbi Jack Riemer*; Introduction by *Rabbi William Cutter*

"Fully engaging in mourning means you will be a different person than before you began." For those who mourn a death, for those who would help them, for those who face a loss of any kind, Brener teaches us the power and strength available to us in the fully experienced mourning process. Guided writing exercises help stimulate the processes of both conscious and unconscious healing.

"A stunning book! It offers an exploration in depth of the place where psychology and religious ritual intersect, and the name of that place is Truth."
> —*Rabbi Harold Kushner, author of* When Bad Things Happen to Good People

7 1/2" x 9", 288 pp. Quality Paperback Original, ISBN 1-879045-23-0 **$19.95**

A TIME TO MOURN, A TIME TO COMFORT
A Guide to Jewish Bereavement and Comfort
by *Dr. Ron Wolfson*

A guide to meeting the needs of those who mourn and those who seek to provide comfort in times of sadness. While this book is written from a layperson's point of view, it also includes the specifics for funeral preparations and practical guidance for preparing the home and family to sit *shiva*.

"A sensitive and perceptive guide to Jewish tradition. Both those who mourn and those who comfort will find it a map to accompany them through the whirlwind."
> —*Deborah E. Lipstadt, Emory University*

7" x 9", 320 pp. Quality Paperback, ISBN 1-879045-96-6 **$16.95**

WHEN A GRANDPARENT DIES
A Kid's Own Remembering Workbook for Dealing with Shiva and the Year Beyond
by *Nechama Liss-Levinson, Ph.D.*

Drawing insights from both psychology and Jewish tradition, this workbook helps children participate in the process of mourning, offering guided exercises, rituals, and places to write, draw, list, create and express their feelings.

"Will bring support, guidance, and understanding for countless children, teachers, and health professionals."
> —*Rabbi Earl A. Grollman, D.D., author of* Talking about Death

8" x 10", 48 pp. Hardcover, illus., 2-color text, ISBN 1-879045-44-3 **$15.95**

LIFE CYCLE...Other books

Bar/Bat Mitzvah Basics: A Practical Family Guide to Coming of Age Together
Ed. by Cantor Helen Leneman 6" x 9", 240 pp, Quality Paperback, ISBN 1-879045-54-0 **$16.95**

Grief in Our Seasons: A Mourner's Kaddish Companion
By Rabbi Kerry Olitzky 4" x 6", 390 pp (est.), Deluxe PB, ISBN 1-879045-55-9 **$18.95**

The New Jewish Baby Book: Names, Ceremonies, Customs—A Guide for Today's Families by Anita Diamant 6" x 9", 328 pp, Quality Paperback, ISBN 1-879045-28-1 **$16.95**

Putting God on the Guest List, 2nd Ed.: How to Reclaim the Spiritual Meaning of Your Child's Bar or Bat Mitzvah by Rabbi Jeffrey K. Salkin 6" x 9", 224 pp, Quality Paperback, ISBN 1-897045-59-1 **$16.95**; HC, ISBN -58-3 **$24.95**

So That Your Values Live On: Ethical Wills & How to Prepare Them
Ed. by Rabbi Jack Riemer & Professor Nathaniel Stampfer 6" x 9", 272 pp. Quality Paperback, ISBN 1-879045-34-6 **$17.95**

Art of Jewish Living Series for Holiday Observance

THE SHABBAT SEDER
by *Dr. Ron Wolfson*

The Shabbat Seder is a concise step-by-step guide designed to teach people the meaning and importance of this weekly celebration, as well as its practices.

Each chapter corresponds to one of ten steps which together comprise the Shabbat dinner ritual, and looks at the *concepts, objects,* and *meanings* behind the specific activity or ritual act. The blessings that accompany the meal are written in both Hebrew and English, and accompanied by English transliteration. Also included are craft projects, recipes, discussion ideas and other creative suggestions for enriching the Shabbat experience.

"A how-to book in the best sense...."
—*Dr. David Lieber, President, University of Judaism, Los Angeles*

7 x 9, 272 pp. Quality Paperback, ISBN 1-879045-90-7 **$16.95**

> Also available are these helpful companions to *The Shabbat Seder*:
> •Booklet of the Blessings and Songs ISBN 1-879045-91-5 $5.00
> •Audiocassette of the Blessings DNO3 $6.00
> •Teacher's Guide ISBN 1-879045-92-3 $4.95

HANUKKAH
by *Dr. Ron Wolfson*
Edited by *Joel Lurie Grishaver*

Designed to help celebrate and enrich the holiday season, *Hanukkah* discusses the holiday's origins, explores the reasons for the Hanukkah candles and customs, and provides everything from recipes to family activities.

There are songs, recipes, useful information on the arts and crafts of Hanukkah, the calendar and its relationship to Christmas time, and games played at Hanukkah. Putting the holiday in a larger, timely context, "December Dilemmas" deals with ways in which a Jewish family can cope with Christmas.

"This book is helpful for the family that strives to induct its members into the spirituality and joys of Jewishness and Judaism...a significant text in the neglected art of Jewish family education."
—*Rabbi Harold M. Schulweis, Cong. Valley Beth Shalom, Encino, CA*

7 x 9, 192 pp. Quality Paperback, ISBN 1-879045-97-4 **$16.95**

THE PASSOVER SEDER
by *Dr. Ron Wolfson*

Explains the concepts behind Passover ritual and ceremony in clear, easy-to-understand language, and offers step-by-step procedures for Passover observance and preparing the home for the holiday.

Easy-to-Follow Format: Using an innovative photo-documentary technique, real families describe in vivid images their own experiences with the Passover holiday. **Easy-to-Read Hebrew Texts:** The Haggadah texts in Hebrew, English, and transliteration are presented in a three-column format designed to help celebrants learn the meaning of the prayers and how to read them. **An Abundance of Useful Information:** A detailed description of how to perform the rituals is included, along with practical questions and answers, and imaginative ideas for Seder celebration.

"A creative 'how-to' for making the Seder a more meaningful experience."
—*Michael Strassfeld, co-author of* The Jewish Catalog

7 x 9, 336 pp. Quality Paperback, ISBN 1-879045-93-1 **$16.95**

> Also available are these helpful companions to *The Passover Seder*:
> •Passover Workbook ISBN 1-879045-94-X $6.95
> •Audiocassette of the Blessings DNO4 $6.00
> •Teacher's Guide ISBN 1-879045-95-8 $4.95

Life Cycle

A HEART OF WISDOM
Making the Jewish Journey from Midlife Through the Elder Years
Edited by *Susan Berrin*

We are all growing older. *A Heart of Wisdom* shows us how to understand our own process of aging—and the aging of those we care about—from a Jewish perspective, from midlife through the elder years.

How does Jewish tradition influence our own aging? How does living, thinking and worshipping as a Jew affect us as we age? How can Jewish tradition help us retain our dignity as we age? Offers insights and enlightenment from Jewish tradition.

"A thoughtfully orchestrated collection of pieces that deal candidly and compassionately with a period of growing concern to us all: midlife through old age."
Chaim Potok

6" x 9", 384 pp. HC, ISBN 1-879045-73-7 **$24.95**

EMBRACING THE COVENANT
Converts to Judaism Talk About Why & How
Edited & with Intros. by *Rabbi Allan L. Berkowitz* and *Patti Moskovitz*

A practical and inspirational companion to the conversion process for Jews-by-Choice and their families. It provides highly personal insights from over 50 people who have made this life-changing decision.

"Passionate, thoughtful and deeply felt personal stories....A wonderful resource, sure to light the way for many who choose to follow the same path."
—*Dru Greenwood, MSW, Director, UAHC-CCAR Commission on Reform Jewish Outreach*

6" x 9", 192 pp. Quality Paperback, ISBN 1-879045-50-8 **$15.95**

LIFECYCLES
V. 1: Jewish Women on Life Passages & Personal Milestones
Ed. and with introductions by *Rabbi Debra Orenstein*
V. 2: Jewish Women on Biblical Themes in Contemporary Life
Ed. and with introductions by
Rabbi Debra Orenstein and *Rabbi Jane Rachel Litman*

This unique three-volume collaboration brings together over one hundred women writers, rabbis, and scholars to create the first comprehensive work on Jewish life cycle that fully includes women's perspectives.

"Nothing is missing from this marvelous collection. You will turn to it for rituals and inspiration, prayer and poetry, comfort and community. *Lifecycles* is a gift to the Jewish woman in America."
—*Letty Cottin Pogrebin, author of* Deborah, Golda, and Me: Being Female and Jewish in America

V. 1: 6 x 9, 480 pp. HC, ISBN 1-879045-14-1, **$24.95**; **V. 2:** 6 x 9, 464 pp. HC, ISBN 1-879045-15-X, **$24.95**

LIFE CYCLE...Other books— The Art of Jewish Living Series for Holiday Observance
by Dr. Ron Wolfson

Hanukkah—7" x 9", 192 pp. Quality Paperback, ISBN 1-879045-97-4 **$16.95**

The Shabbat Seder—7" x 9", 272 pp, Quality Paperback, ISBN 1-879045-90-7 **$16.95**; Booklet of Blessings **$5.00**; Audiocassette of Blessings **$6.00**; Teacher's Guide **$4.95**

The Passover Seder—7" x 9", 272 pp, Quality Paperback, ISBN 1-879045-90-7 **$16.95**; Passover Workbook, **$6.95**; Audiocassette of Blessings, **$6.00**; Teacher's Guide, **$4.95**

Children's Spirituality

A PRAYER FOR THE EARTH
The Story of Naamah, Noah's Wife

For ages 4-8

by *Sandy Eisenberg Sasso*
Full color illustrations by *Bethanne Andersen*

NONSECTARIAN, NONDENOMINATIONAL.

This new story, based on an ancient text, opens readers' religious imaginations to new ideas about the well-known story of the Flood. When God tells Noah to bring the animals of the world onto the ark, God *also* calls on Naamah, Noah's wife, to save each plant on Earth.

> "A lovely tale....Children of all ages should be drawn to this parable for our times."
> —*Tomie dePaola, artist/author of books for children*

•AWARD WINNER•

9" x 12", 32 pp. Hardcover, Full color illus., ISBN 1-879045-60-5 **$16.95**

THE 11TH COMMANDMENT
Wisdom from Our Children

For all ages

by The Children of America

MULTICULTURAL, NONSECTARIAN, NONDENOMINATIONAL.

"If there were an Eleventh Commandment, what would it be?"

Children of many religious denominations across America answer this question—in their own drawings and words—in *The 11th Commandment*.

> "Wonderful....This unusual book provides both food for thought and insight into the hopes and fears of today's young."
> —*American Library Association's* Booklist

8" x 10", 48 pp. Hardcover, Full color illus., ISBN 1-879045-46-X **$16.95**

SHARING BLESSINGS
Children's Stories for Exploring the Spirit of the Jewish Holidays

For ages 6-10

by *Rahel Musleah* and *Rabbi Michael Klayman*
Full color illustrations by *Mary O'Keefe Young*

What is the spiritual message of each of the Jewish holidays? How do we teach it to our children?

Many books tell children about the historical significance and customs of the holidays. Now, through engaging, creative stories about one family's spiritual preparation, *Sharing Blessings* explores ways to get into the *spirit* of 13 different holidays.

> "A beguiling introduction to important Jewish values by way of the holidays."
> —*Rabbi Harold Kushner, author of* When Bad Things Happen to Good People *and* How Good Do We Have to Be?

7" x 10", 64 pp. Hardcover, Full color illus., ISBN 1-879045-71-0 **$18.95**

THE BOOK OF MIRACLES
A Young Person's Guide to Jewish Spiritual Awareness

For ages 9-13

by *Lawrence Kushner*

With a Special 10th Anniversary Introduction and all new illustrations by the author.

From the miracle at the Red Sea to the miracle of waking up this morning, this intriguing book introduces kids to a way of everyday spiritual thinking to last a lifetime. Kushner, whose award-winning books have brought spirituality to life for countless adults, now shows young people how to use Judaism as a foundation on which to build their lives.

6" x 9", 96 pp. Hardcover, 2-color illus., ISBN 1-879045-78-8 **$16.95**

Children's Spirituality

For ages 8 and up

BUT GOD REMEMBERED
Stories of Women from Creation to the Promised Land
by *Sandy Eisenberg Sasso*
Full color illustrations by *Bethanne Andersen*

NONSECTARIAN, NONDENOMINATIONAL.

A fascinating collection of four different stories of women only briefly mentioned in biblical tradition and religious texts, but never before explored. Award-winning author Sasso brings to life the intriguing stories of Lilith, Serach, Bityah, and the Daughters of Z, courageous and strong women from ancient tradition. All teach important values through their faith and actions.

•AWARD WINNER•

"Exquisite....a book of beauty, strength and spirituality."
—*Association of Bible Teachers*

9" x 12", 32 pp. Hardcover, Full color illus., ISBN 1-879045-43-5 **$16.95**

•AWARD WINNER•

IN GOD'S NAME
by *Sandy Eisenberg Sasso*
Full color illustrations by *Phoebe Stone*

For ages 4-8

MULTICULTURAL, NONSECTARIAN, NONDENOMINATIONAL.

Like an ancient myth in its poetic text and vibrant illustrations, this modern fable about the search for God's name celebrates the diversity and, at the same time, the unity of all the people of the world. Each seeker claims he or she alone knows the answer. Finally, they come together and learn what God's name really is, sharing the ultimate harmony of belief in one God by people of all faiths, all backgrounds.

"I got goose bumps when I read *In God's Name,* its language and illustrations are that moving. This is a book children will love and the whole family will cherish for its beauty and power."
—*Francine Klagsbrun, author of* Mixed Feelings: Love, Hate, Rivalry, and Reconciliation among Brothers and Sisters

"What a lovely, healing book!"
—*Madeleine L'Engle*

> Selected by
> Parent Council Ltd.™

9" x 12", 32 pp. Hardcover, Full color illus., ISBN 1-879045-26-5 **$16.95**

For ages 4-8

GOD'S PAINTBRUSH
by *Sandy Eisenberg Sasso*
Full color illustrations by *Annette Compton*

MULTICULTURAL, NONSECTARIAN, NONDENOMINATIONAL.

Invites children of all faiths and backgrounds to encounter God openly in their own lives. Wonderfully interactive, provides questions adult and child can explore together at the end of each episode.

•AWARD WINNER•

"An excellent way to honor the imaginative breadth and depth of the spiritual life of the young."
—*Dr. Robert Coles, Harvard University*

11" x 8 1/2", 32 pp. Hardcover, Full color illus., ISBN 1-879045-22-2 **$16.95**

Also Available!
Teacher's Guide: A Guide for Jewish & Christian Educators and Parents
8 1/2" x 11", 32 pp. Paperback, ISBN 1-879045-57-5 **$6.95**

AVAILABLE FROM BETTER BOOKSTORES.
TRY YOUR BOOKSTORE FIRST.

Order Information

# of Copies	Book Title / ISBN (Last 3 digits)	$ Amount
_____	_____	_____
_____	_____	_____
_____	_____	_____
_____	_____	_____
_____	_____	_____
_____	_____	_____
_____	_____	_____
_____	_____	_____
_____	_____	_____
_____	_____	_____
_____	_____	_____
_____	_____	_____
_____	_____	_____
_____	_____	_____
_____	_____	_____

For shipping/handling, add $3.50 for the first book, $2.00 each
add'l book (to a max of $15.00) $ S/H _____

TOTAL _____

Check enclosed for $_____ *payable to:* JEWISH LIGHTS Publishing

Charge my credit card: ❏ MasterCard   ❏ Visa

Credit Card #_____Expires _____

Signature _____Phone (_____)_____

Your Name _____

Street_____

City / State / Zip _____

Ship To:

Name _____

Street_____

City / State / Zip _____

Phone, fax or mail to: **JEWISH LIGHTS Publishing**
P.O. Box 237 • Sunset Farm Offices, Route 4 • Woodstock, Vermont 05091
Tel (802) 457-4000   Fax (802) 457-4004   www.jewishlights.com
Credit card orders **(800) 962-4544** (9AM–5PM ET Monday–Friday)
Generous discounts on quantity orders. SATISFACTION GUARANTEED. Prices subject to change.